LUCID DREAMING

PLAIN AND SIMPLE

LUCID DREAMING

PLAIN AND SIMPLE

TIPS *and* TECHNIQUES *for* INSIGHT, CREATIVITY, *and* PERSONAL GROWTH

Robert Waggoner & Caroline McCready

Conari Press

First published in 2015 by Conari Press, an imprint of
Red Wheel/Weiser, LLC
With offices at:
665 Third Street, Suite 400
San Francisco, CA 94107
www.redwheelweiser.com

ISBN: 978-1-57324-641-5

Library of Congress Cataloging-in-Publication Data available upon request.

Cover design by Jim Warner
Interior by Frame25 Productions
Typeset in Adobe Garamond Pro

Printed in Canada.
MAR
10 9   8 7 6 5 4 3 2 1

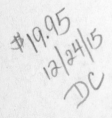

CONTENTS

ACKNOWLEDGMENTS

We wish to acknowledge and thank the many lucid dreamers, researchers, and others who provided helpful insights, lucid dreams, and editing for this book. Their contributions have made this a much richer and deeper exploration of lucid dreaming.

Although Cicero cautioned that "it is difficult to remember all and ungracious to omit any," we want to mention specifically the following lucid dreamers for their assistance and support: Don Middendorf, Ph.D.; Ed Kellogg, Ph.D.; Clare Johnson, Ph.D.; Lucy Gillis; Maria Isabel Pita; Beverly D'Urso, Ph.D.; Charlie Morley; Ian Burke; Caz Coronel; Tereza Griffin; John D. Cooper; Dr. Rory Mac Sweeney; Olga Richterova; Mary Ziemer; Joy Fatooh; Kristin E. LaMarca, Ph.D.; Line Salvesen; Robert J. Hoss; Dr. Scott Sparrow; David L. Kahn; Kelly Frappier; PasQuale Ourtane; Justina Lasley; Nigel Hamilton, Ph.D.; Linda Mastrangelo; Melanie Schädlich; Jeffrey Peck, Mark Hettmannczyk; Daniel Love; Jane Ahring; Rebecca Turner; Ryan Hurd; and various unnamed others.

We also wish to thank the researchers who continue to explore and support research efforts in lucid dreaming. The extraordinary efforts of pioneers like Keith Hearne, Ph.D.; Alan Worsley; and Stephen LaBerge, Ph.D., have laid a strong foundation for current researchers and assisted countless lucid dreamers.

Special thanks to artist and lucid dreamer Dustyn Lucas for allowing us to include an image of his painting, *The Mirage of Duality in the Sands of Time*, which he originally saw in a lucid dream. To see more of his work, visit his website at *www.dustynlucas.com*. Also thanks to Justina Lasley for allowing us to excerpt a dream interpretation technique from her book, *Honoring the Dream*. We very much appreciate the use of written excerpts by Ed Kellogg and author Maria Isabel Pita. The insights of Ed Kellogg on healing in lucid dreams and the phenomenology of this state have given us a broader and wiser view. Finally, we send our deep thanks to Don Middendorf and Jeffrey Peck for reviewing and improving the final manuscript.

Sincere thanks to our many friends and colleagues who supported and encouraged us in this process. In particular, Robert wishes to thank the International Association for the Study of Dreams and its members, who provide a welcoming and thoughtful place to explore the depths of dreaming and the lucid dream experience. In addition, he thanks his family and his wife, Wendy, for all of their support and encouragement.

Caroline wishes to thank all the people who come to her lucid dreaming groups and workshops in London. She also thanks Charlie Morley, whose lucid dreaming forums have been an ongoing source of encouragement and inspiration, and Debbie Winterbourne for her insight and help in creating a community of lucid dreamers in London. Caroline extends a very special thank you for the endless support from her treasured family and beautiful friends, especially her parents and brother, and Tereza, Zakia, Emma, Caz, and Hannah.

A portion of the authors' royalties from this book are being donated to *www.replanttrees.org*.

PREFACE

In 1975, I taught myself how to lucid dream (or realize I was dreaming while in the dream state) and have logged more than 1,000 lucid dreams since that time. Because my first book, *Lucid Dreaming: Gateway to the Inner Self,* explores the incredible experience and potential of lucid dreaming, many people have asked for a simple how-to book on inducing, stabilizing, and working within lucid dreams.

A few years ago in London, I met a talented artist, speaker, and lucid dreamer named Caroline McCready, who agreed to join me in creating a guidebook on lucid dreaming to assist others on this path. Having another set of experiences and insights, like Caroline's, has done much to enhance the depth and richness of this guide, particularly in chapters 1, 11, 12, and 13.

In this book, we have sought to provide the necessary tools for you to have lucid dreams and investigate this extraordinary state firsthand. Here, along with instructions distilled from many years of personal experience, you will find valuable insights and techniques from our lucid dreaming colleagues and friends.

Please focus on this guide carefully and do not rush through it, because, when you realize you are dreaming and become lucidly aware, you will need to recall and apply these tips and techniques.

Lucid dreaming exists as a mentally dynamic state and often reflects back to us our beliefs, assumptions, feelings, and expectations. As you venture into lucid dreaming more deeply, you will realize that the exploration encourages you to examine certain beliefs and assumptions more critically. In fact, you may come to experience another type of education through lucid dreaming—an education in the nature of the mind and perceived experience that calls forth insights capable of transforming yourself and your waking life.

As an introduction to lucid dreaming, this book does not address many advanced topics, including cultural assumptions about the nature and meaning of dreaming and lucid dreaming. In future books by us and others, we hope these areas and assumptions will receive more attention and investigation.

Best wishes on your journey of awareness,
Robert Waggoner and Caroline McCready
January 2014

INTRODUCTION

To understand lucid dreaming more clearly, it often helps to have others tell their stories of how they were introduced to the idea of becoming consciously aware of dreaming while in the dream state. Here in the Introduction, coauthor Caroline McCready and I recount our own discovery of lucid dreaming's depth and a bit about the lessons we learned.

Caroline's Experience

I can still remember my first lucid dream vividly. As the dream begins, I am in a small room playing a game of pool with my cousin when I suddenly realized that I was dreaming. As soon as I realized it was a dream, I felt astounded. Knowing that I was actually *inside* a dream was mind-blowing. Everything felt so real. When I ran my fingertips over the green felt on the table, it felt realistically soft and fibrous. The pool balls felt so convincingly solid and smooth. They made very real clinking sounds as they hit one another. I remember stopping and becoming very still, just wanting to take it all in, in complete wonder. Then I woke up.

I started to glimpse the potential of lucid dreaming when I became lucid for a second time. In this next dream, I found myself playing by a swing in a very accurate replica of my real garden. Something triggered my lucidity and led me to an exciting lucid dream. In waking life, I had recently watched the first *Superman* film with Christopher Reeve. In my dream, I suddenly recalled the scene in which he takes Lois Lane flying. Lucidly aware, I thought to myself that that would be amazing! No sooner had I thought this than a dream version of Superman, in his blue-and-red caped suit, came swooping in and flew me up above my garden. I remember looking down as my swing became smaller and smaller and my garden became increasingly distant. It felt so exhilarating!

In the many lucid flying dreams to follow, I subsequently discovered I didn't need Superman to fly me around at all, since I could soar like a bird solo. I regularly flew over valleys, rivers, and mountains. My favorite place to fly became Lake Louise in Canada, where my family used to visit whenever we went to see my Canadian father's family in Alberta. I loved Canada, and it felt amazing to be able to visit realistic dream replicas of places there, let alone fly over these magnificent landscapes. I always woke up feeling exhilarated, almost able to feel where the wind had brushed my cheeks.

As I grew into a teenager, these experiences became less and less frequent; and, as an adult, my lucid dreams became completely sporadic. I so desperately wanted to fly again that, on the rare occasions when lucidity sparked within a dream, I hurriedly and excitedly started to fly, but I almost always drifted out of lucidity into a normal dream within mere moments. It was frustrating and, eventually, my lucid adventures became fond, but distant, memories.

Many years later, I started having intensely vivid dreams. They were so vivid that it was as if they were popping out of my head every morning, begging to be written down. So I revisited my childhood practice of keeping a daily dream journal and became interested in dream interpretation. Lucid dreaming re-entered my awareness and I purchased two books about it—Robert's first book and Stephen LaBerge's introduction to lucid dreaming. When younger, I had completely spontaneous lucid dreams and had no idea that you could actually prompt lucidity. Reading that I could purposefully induce lucid dreams thrilled me. More important, I felt astonished by the scope and breadth of lucid dream experiences. You can question dream characters, uncover hidden subconscious limitations, fulfill all kinds of desires, and—most curious to me—explore the nature of consciousness itself.

Returning to lucid dreaming was like rediscovering a lost love for me. But now I could explore it in ways I had never imagined possible. I excitedly devoured the books and started practicing all the techniques. I drew little prompts on my hands to help me question my reality (a lucid dreaming technique), repetitively performed reality checks, and thought about lucid dreaming constantly. I absolutely immersed myself in it.

My first induced lucid dream came two weeks after I started practicing the techniques. On this particular night, I slept restlessly. About four o'clock in the morning, I felt unable to get back to sleep. I decided to get up and meditate, hoping this would remedy my insomnia. It did help enormously, and I soon drifted soundly back to sleep. I then found myself looking after two children in a strange room. The interior of the room looked like the outside of a viewing enclosure in a zoo. Rather than standing outside looking in, however, I saw that we were the ones enclosed. When I tried to open the windows, I noticed there was just a solid brick wall and no apparent means for escape. Being in a room without doors or windows had been a common lucidity trigger for me when younger, and again I realized that this was a dream. I told the kids to follow me and I created an imaginary door in the brick that opened to bright sunshine. We found ourselves in a beautiful countryside. I met a lovely, responsible-looking dream character to look after the kids so that I could go and explore the dream.

I won't go into all the details because it covered seven pages of my dream journal. Among other things, however, I revisited my childhood love and went flying over Lake Louise in Canada once more; I played around with manifesting light in an old, empty house; I examined curious objects in the drawers of an old-fashioned apothecary; I spoke to various dream characters; and I got up to general mischief with a dream version of a friend from Sydney whom I hadn't seen for a while in waking reality. The lucid dream felt as if it lasted well over an hour. In fact, at one point, I was on a grassy bank by a river where there were many dream figures sitting and enjoying the beautiful, peaceful surroundings. When I tried to talk to them, they expressed annoyance that I'd been lucid for so long because they were getting tired of it!

Because of my deep interest, I started to have lucid experiences almost every morning—and often multiple experiences in a single morning. I found myself frequently entering a lucid dream directly from early-morning meditations, which seemed incredible and almost surreal. I felt as if I had discovered a treasure trove for my inquiring mind to explore: an adventure playground limited only by my imagination.

I have witnessed my life, as well as my reaction to life, transformed in so many positive ways by the insights gained from dreams and lucid dreams. Sadly, our culture largely ignores dreams. By losing touch with dreaming, however, we have lost touch with an amazing tool for understanding ourselves and life itself. In Robert's first book, he makes this analogy:

> No sailor controls the sea. Only a foolish sailor would say such a thing. Similarly, no lucid dreamer controls the dream. Like a sailor on the sea, we lucid dreamers direct our perceptual awareness within the larger state of dreaming.[1]

I think this is a beautiful analogy. Dreams are vast and always in motion; going against the tide of a dream can be difficult, and standing still can feel like treading water against waves constantly in motion. We don't consciously create our dreams; we only ride their waves and direct our experience. In this way, lucid dreaming can also be compared to surfing. I lived in Australia for two and a half years, near the popular surfing beaches of Manly and Bondi. I met many surfers there and one thing that always struck me was just how much surfers respect the ocean. Just as I have never met a surfer who hasn't developed a deep respect for the ocean, I have yet to meet an experienced lucid dreamer who doesn't have a similar deep respect for dreams.

Some people express concern that focusing on dreaming may perhaps prevent lucid dreamers from truly living in the present, and may perhaps be used as an escape from normal life. My experience has been the opposite. Through lucid dreaming, I feel as if I wake up more fully in my waking life as well as in my dreams. We spend so much of our time thinking about the past or mulling over potential future events that to be awake is to embrace the present moment fully. Lucid dreaming techniques and lucid dreams teach us to be in the now, fully and positively, in both our waking and dreaming lives.

Lucid dreams continue to entertain, aid, and teach me. I feel so grateful for this amazing tool and the opportunity to share these insights with others. I feel passionately about helping others gain lucidity in every respect.

Robert's Experience

At the beginning of 1981, I recall sitting in my university's library reading a *Psychology Today* article by Stephen LaBerge that announced scientific evidence for lucid dreaming. I felt amazed, relieved, and happy. Finally! Finally, some researcher had devised a way to validate the existence of lucid dreaming.

Six years earlier, I had become successful at inducing lucid dreams by using a certain pre-sleep technique (see chapter 3). Each time I realized that I was dreaming and became consciously aware, I had a sudden sense of lucid euphoria. The sudden shift of consciousness made me feel more real, more aware, more vast. Engaging the reality of the dream experience while consciously knowing, "This is a dream!" felt joyfully surreal.

I stumbled into this field as a true novice. Yet by the time of LaBerge's article, I had experienced more than 100 lucid dreams. However, when I tried to discuss this fascinating phenomenon with others, most people either replied that I "had simply had a dream of dreaming" or just dismissed the whole thing as impossible. Now with LaBerge's research, my experiences of lucid dreaming appeared fundamentally valid and scientifically acceptable.

In those early years, lucid dreaming existed in a kind of informational wilderness. I had virtually no other lucid dreamers to whom I could talk, no one from whom to get advice, and no one with whom to share my discoveries. Most of my discoveries—my lessons in lucidity—came after careful analysis of one of my own instructive lucid dreams or one of my own many educational failures. The little material available by authors before 1981—like that by Patricia Garfield, Ann Faraday, Carlos Castaneda, and Celia Green—provided only brief sketches of what to do and how to do it. Nevertheless, the beauty and wonder of lucid dreaming had hooked me like a visit to some tropical island, and I looked forward to returning there as often as I could.

Initially, the sensed reality of lucid dreams stunned me. When lucidly aware, you can examine the detail of dream objects. You can smile when you turn over a dinner plate at a dream restaurant and see the pottery stamp, even though you know that this exists as a dream dinner plate. In a lucid dream, you can stop and feel the soft, cottony touch of a dream T-shirt, amazed that it feels exactly like the waking version. Comparing and contrasting lucid reality with waking reality proves a constant amusement to you.

Although, to me, lucid dreaming seemed like a type of inner reality that mimicked the waking one, I found that it followed a set of different rules and principles. I spent many lucid dreams joyfully free from gravity, flying around and amusing myself, but careful not to get too excited or stare at anything for too long (two rules that most lucid dreamers learn by trial and error). Still, in this playful use of lucid dreams, I learned how to focus and concentrate my mind better. I learned how to use the powers of expectation and belief constructively, and how to engage my intent. Looking back, perhaps the best thing that I could have done involved play—playing with my lucid dreams until finally I began to see the relationship between my conscious mindset, the dream experience and the supportively aware subconscious.

After 1981, things began to change. Articles on lucid dreaming appeared periodically in national magazines. A little magazine, *Dream Network Bulletin*, emerged and offered lucid dreamers a place to share experiences and techniques. By mail, I reached out to other lucid dreamers. Slowly, it dawned on me that people's experience of lucid dreaming showed common features and principles. Although the dream content and symbols of each experience seemed unique to each dreamer, a consistent framework of rules and principles existed beneath the lucid dream events. This hidden framework suggested that dreaming and the unconscious actually followed rules and had structure. Scientists who claimed that dreams amounted to chaos and the random firing of neurons thus understood little about its principled nature—a structure that lucid dreamers around the world seemed to discover naturally and on which they agree.

As I began to grasp the principles of lucid dreaming more clearly, it became much easier for me to remain lucidly aware. Previously, like most lucid dreamers, I struggled to stay lucid as I fought against breaking the rules and being tossed out of the dream or losing my awareness and returning to normal dreaming. As my lucid dreams got longer, it became easier to explore more deeply and even to conduct small experiments.

The big turning point for me came ten years into my lucid dreaming practice. Around that time, I joined a group of talented lucid dreamers who sought to conduct one experiment each month over the course of three years. Each month, we attempted individual experiments and sent the results to the organizer, who photocopied the reports and mailed them back out to the entire group. In March 1985, we had a simple experimental goal—to find out what the characters in our lucid dream represented.

In my own experiment, I became lucid as I entered a building and followed a woman into an office setting. Standing there, I recalled the month's experimental goal and looked around at the four dream figures. I decided to approach an older man in a three-piece suit and I put the question to him very simply: "What do you represent?" At that moment, a very strange thing happened. From above him, a voice boomed out: "The acquired characteristics!" A bit surprised by this voice from above and its incomplete answer, I asked: "The acquired characteristics of what?" The source of the voice seemed to process my query for a moment, and then boomed out: "The acquired characteristics of the happy giver!" I decided that I had accomplished my goal of finding out what a dream figure represents, so I told myself to wake up.

In the morning, I recalled a disturbing incident from the day before in which I had talked to a woman at a charity. This woman told me that the only reason people gave to her organization was to get their names in the annual list of donors. As I walked away from her, I wryly thought: "The lord loves a happy giver!" This dream figure thus seemed to represent symbolically a bit of day residue from my waking reality.

However, something profound happened in that lucid dream. For the first time, I wondered whether an intelligent awareness existed behind our dreams. Following up on my curiosity, I began the practice of ignoring dream figures in subsequent lucid dreams and simply addressing questions and requests to this invisible, hidden awareness. Incredibly, the awareness behind the dream responded. From that moment, lucid dreaming became much more than a mental playground or simplistic virtual reality for me; it offered me a path to investigate the broader nature of the psyche. Lucid dreaming showed its potential to become a revolutionary tool for personal and scientific inner exploration.

Chapter 1

THE SCIENCE AND PARADOX OF LUCID DREAMING

In very simple terms, lucid dreaming means realizing that you are dreaming while in the dream state. The American Psychological Association has a more official definition in its 2007 *Dictionary of Psychology*, defining a lucid dream as "a dream in which the sleeper is aware that he or she is dreaming and may be able to influence the progress of the dream narrative."

Both of these definitions identify the fundamental paradoxical quality of lucid dreaming: the knowledge and realization that you are consciously aware within the dream state. In fact, when you become lucidly aware within a dream, you may even find yourself announcing: "Wait, this is a dream. I am dreaming!"

My very first lucid dream occurred spontaneously around age 11 or 12 when I found myself in the book stacks of the public library and saw a *Tyrannosaurus rex* walking through the aisles. At first, I felt alarmed, but then I thought: "Wait a second, dinosaurs are extinct." And at that moment, I realized: "This must be a dream!" I knew I was dreaming, even as I dreamed. Even in this short example, you see the active components of most lucid dreams:

- Observing or experiencing something unusual (e.g., *Tyrannosaurus rex*)

- Critically reflecting on or analyzing the experience (e.g., dinosaurs are extinct)

• Concluding that "dreaming" represents the most likely explanation (e.g., "This must be a dream!")

Essentially, lucid dreaming shows the triumphant emergence of your reflective awareness; you awaken to an understanding of your actual situation. Now consider how you often act in regular dreams. You accept things. You go along with whatever happens. You make up stories to justify your actions and the events. You lack higher levels of critical awareness and analysis. So when you see *Tyrannosaurus rex*, you normally feel fear and run away. In regular dreams, you accept incredible situations because of your diminished critical awareness.

Tibetan Buddhists have a wonderful metaphor for dreaming. They liken the experience of regular dreaming to that of a blind horse with a lame rider. In this metaphor, the lame rider is the person's largely unaware mind, which sits on a blind horse that dashes around with little control. If the rider (the person's mind) overcomes its lameness and becomes lucidly aware, then it can begin to direct the blind horse (the energy of the dream) and use it for personal transformation and spiritual growth.

Much of this book focuses on techniques and practices that you can use to elevate your awareness and critical reflection about your waking experience. By doing the practices given here, you can increase your chances of becoming lucidly aware in the dream state. In fact, many people report that just reading and thinking about becoming aware in the dream state has been enough to prompt them to become lucid in tonight's dreaming.

When you realize in a dream that you are dreaming, you have become lucidly aware. At that moment, you can do many amazing things:

• You can consciously decide what actions to perform.

• You can become free of waking-state limitations. You can fly like Superman, perform magic like Harry Potter, walk through concrete walls, breathe underwater, seek creative solutions to waking issues, and much more.

• You can interact and converse with dream figures.

- You can conduct personal and scientific experiments.

- You can begin to explore the dream space and the contents of your unconscious.

- You can work on improving waking skills for sports, business, and more.

Although these examples hint at lucid dreaming's possibilities, the greater potential of lucid dreaming for individuals, science, and society seems truly staggering and will be more fully discussed later in this chapter.

Evidence for Lucid Dreaming

The scientific evidence for lucid dreaming reveals an amazing story of insight, talent, and ingenuity. In the mid-1970s, Keith Hearne, a graduate student studying sleep and dreams at the University of Hull in England, met Alan Worsley, who claimed to have frequent lucid dreams. Hearne listened to him and was intrigued. Being a scientist, he spent time pondering how he could create an acceptable experiment to provide scientific evidence for lucid dreaming.

Later, a brilliant solution came to him. During sleep, our bodies become functionally paralyzed. But while dreaming, researchers have shown that we usually have rapid eye movement (REM). Hearne wondered whether a lucid dreamer could use his eyes to signal that he was lucidly aware and conscious while dreaming. If this were possible, it would create a major breakthrough for the sciences of dreaming, consciousness, and psychology.

So Hearne brought Worsley into the sleep lab and put polygraph pads on his eyes to record his rapid eye movements while dreaming. He then instructed Worsley to move his eyes left and right a pre-determined number of times when he became lucidly aware in a dream.

In April 1975, it happened. Sleeping in the lab, Worsley realized he was dreaming and became lucidly aware. Then he recalled the experimental design and moved his eyes left and right a pre-determined number of times to show that he was consciously aware and lucidly dreaming.[2] Other measurements in the sleep lab confirmed that his body remained asleep, although his mind was consciously aware and signaling with the prearranged eye movements. When Hearne saw the hard evidence of the pre-arranged REM eye movements, he later remarked: "It was like getting signals from another world. Philosophically, scientifically, it was simply mind blowing."[3]

Separately, in the United States almost three years later, Stephen LaBerge, a Stanford University doctoral student and lucid dreamer, wondered how a scientist could provide evidence for lucid dreaming. Like Hearne, he realized that a lucid dreamer could signal by moving his eyes in a pre-arranged pattern. Placing himself in the sleep lab in 1978, LaBerge became lucidly aware in a dream and signaled his awareness by moving his eyes left to right a few times, which was recorded by the laboratory equipment. He replicated this eye-signal verification technique in twenty subsequent nights in the sleep lab.[4]

After the scientific paper he wrote describing his research was rejected by the prestigious journal *Science*—one reviewer adamantly refused to believe it possible to become lucidly aware in the dream state—and then by *Nature*—which did not review the study, but judged the topic "not of sufficient general interest"—LaBerge succeeded in getting his research published in an acceptable, peer-reviewed journal.[5] He then became closely connected to this fascinating new area of scientific exploration and headed much of the subsequent research into it.

How to Identify Lucid Dreams

Now that you understand the definition of lucid dreaming, have you had a lucid dream? If so, take a moment to write out your first lucid dream or a lucid dream that you remember. Now, write down a typical dream. Compare the lucid dream to the typical dream. How do the dreams differ after you become lucid?

The Neurology of Lucid Dreaming

What does the brain look like when someone is lucid dreaming? And what may that tell us about the nature of awareness—both dream awareness and waking awareness?

In the past ten years, subjects have been studied while lucid dreaming in fMRI machines (wearing special headphones to mute the machine's noise so they can remain asleep) and separately while wearing 19-channel electroencephalogram (EEG) receptors on their scalps. Both studies provided similar evidence about brain function during lucid dreaming.

In very general terms, the researchers discovered that, when you lucid dream, the parts of your brain associated with dreaming show their usual activity; but certain parts of your brain normally associated with waking consciousness also show activity (e.g., frontal and fronto-lateral portions of the brain). Essentially, your brain activity confirms what lucid dreamers experience—you engage a dream scene knowing it as a dream and can consciously direct and manipulate your thought process. In essence, you have conscious awareness within a dream that you are dreaming.

The research team led by Ursula Voss that performed the 19-channel EEG recording of the lucid dream state concluded "... [L]ucid dreaming constitutes a hybrid state of consciousness with definable and measurable differences from waking and from REM sleep, particularly in frontal areas."[6] It also commented: "Because lucidity can be self-induced, it constitutes not only an opportunity to study the brain basis of conscious states but also demonstrates how a voluntary intervention can change those states." In the team's view, lucid dreaming shows us a special neurological state between the waking and dreaming states, but with features of both states existing simultaneously.

A member of the other research team that performed the combined EEG/fMRI study, Michael Czisch at the Max Planck Institute of Psychiatry, commented to *Science Daily* about that team's research results:

> The general basic activity of the brain is similar in a normal dream and in a lucid dream. . . . In a lucid state, however, the activity in certain areas of the cerebral cortex increases markedly within seconds. The involved areas of the cerebral

cortex are the right dorsolateral prefrontal cortex to which, commonly, the function of self-assessment is attributed, and the frontopolar regions, which are responsible for evaluating our own thoughts and feelings. The precuneus is also especially active, a part of the brain that has long been linked with self-perception.[7]

Using the fMRI data, this research team could focus on the specific areas within the brain that showed activity. The results clearly showed that lucid dreaming activated parts of the cerebral cortex connected with self-assessment, self-perception, and examination of thoughts and feelings.[8]

This neurological research basically confirmed the thousand-plus-year contention of lucid dreamers: 1) Through voluntary actions, you can achieve lucid awareness in the dream state, 2) When lucid, you have the capacity for metacognition or awareness about your own thought process, 3) When lucid, you can direct your actions within that unique state of dreaming, and 4) When lucid, you can assess your actions and learn from the response.

Science has barely investigated the extraordinary potential of this state to develop skills, seek creativity, effect physical changes, and obtain psychological insights. In fairness though, the research funds devoted to lucid dreaming seem extremely small, relative to the potential for scientific contributions. Nevertheless, as the number of lucid dreamers continues to increase and experienced lucid dreamers gain even more insights, the depth of these personal experiments and conceptual explorations will likely grow, as will the reports of fascinating achievements.

How Common Is Lucid Dreaming?

The *International Journal of Dream Research* has published studies on lucid dreaming surveys of students in numerous countries. When college psychology students were asked whether they had ever become aware that they were dreaming while in a dream (i.e., lucid dreaming), the researchers[9] reported these results for positive responses:

- 71 percent in the United States

- 82 percent in Germany

- 73 percent in the Netherlands

- 47 percent in Japan

The research surveys shows that about 20 percent of college-age lucid dreamers claim to have frequent lucid dreams (that is, at least one each month). Our impression is that, if you ask deeply interested lucid dreamers who routinely visit lucid dream forums about the frequency of their lucid dreaming, a majority average about one to eight lucid dreams per month, with occasional periods of inactivity. Considering that we have five or more dreams a night, or about 150 dreams each month, the percentage of dreams that are lucid seems relatively small.

Research has also shown the prevalence of lucid dreaming among younger students. One study by Michael Schredl and others, *Lucid Dreaming in Children: The UK Library Study*, described how researchers placed surveys on dreaming in libraries in the United Kingdom and received 3,579 responses from children ages six to eighteen years. When asked whether they had experienced a lucid dream at least once, 43.5 percent responded affirmatively.[10]

A more in-depth 2012 study published in the *Journal of Sleep Research* dealt with 694 German students in primary and secondary schools between the ages of six and nineteen. Led by researcher Ursula Voss, this study investigated the hypothesis "that lucid dreaming occurs primarily in childhood and puberty." It found that "lucid dreaming is quite pronounced in young children . . ." Indeed, around 51 percent of these young people reported a lucid dream.[11]

Using a questionnaire and one-on-one interviews, Voss's research team asked the children to provide examples of dreams in which they became aware of dreaming. They received examples like the following:

- **Narrative 1** (boy, age 7): I dreamt I was playing soccer with my friends, and when I looked at my legs I saw that they were distorted. Then I realized it must be a dream because they did not at all look like my own legs. Then I looked up and saw that I was in a giant soccer stadium and I was able to play with my favorite soccer team (the adult team). I could run real fast, faster than in waking.

- **Narrative 3** (girl, age 10): Someone was haunting me. And I was with my girlfriend. The chaser stood before me and wanted to kill me. And then I realized it was only a dream. So I made the person disappear and then suddenly it wasn't dark anymore.

The researchers note that many of these students exhibited an ability to influence the course of the dream, even though "these students had no training and lucid dreaming occurred spontaneously." Often, when they became lucid, they reported using the experience to go flying or to deal with threatening situations.

If you have children, grandchildren, nieces, or nephews, ask them whether they have ever become aware of dreaming while in a dream state. You may be surprised by how many have had a lucid dream.

When research studies by Jayne Gackenbach investigated personality and gender differences in lucid dreaming, at first it appeared that women had a distinct advantage over men. When the data was examined more deeply, however, it showed that women reported more dreams overall than men—hence more lucid dreams as well. When an adjustment was made for this quantitative distinction, the gender difference largely disappeared. Nonetheless, lucid dream reports seem positively associated with strong dream recall.[12]

Additional research by Gackenbach indicates that people with good spatial skills and field independence have some advantage in becoming lucid.[13] The *APA Dictionary of Psychology* defines field independence as "a cognitive style in which the individual consistently relies more on internal referents (body sensation cues) than on external referents (environmental cues)." In lucid dreams, we often deal with unusual situations and changing space perspectives, so a reliance on our inner felt sense of direction supports us as we maneuver within dreaming.

When Robert interviews talented lucid dreamers for the quarterly magazine *Lucid Dreaming Experience*, he occasionally asks about their first experience with lucid dreaming. He has discovered that a small number began lucid dreaming around age five. (Most report their first lucid dream occurring in their pre-teen to teenage years.) Normally, they recall this early date because they used lucid dreaming to handle recurring childhood nightmares.

For example, a Norwegian lucid dreamer, Line Salvesen, reported feeling amazed when reading about lucid dreaming for the first time in a Norwegian magazine; she assumed that was how everyone dreamed! In her case, she recalls becoming lucidly aware as a small child in order to deal with recurring nightmares. After that, she found it easy to become lucidly aware each night in almost every dream. Now, she uses her skill to help researchers investigate lucid dreaming in the sleep lab.[14]

Cases also exist of people learning to lucid dream at a more mature age. In another issue of *Lucid Dreaming Experience*, Robert interviewed a man named Tad Messenger, who experienced his first lucid dream at age fifty-two. He reports having relatively frequent lucid dreams thereafter. His skill at lucid dreaming developed after persevering through a lengthy psycho-spiritual practice. Then, he claims, "it was like a door opened," and he could often become lucid when he had the intent to do so.[15]

German researchers Melanie Schädlich and Daniel Erlacher investigated how lucid dreamers applied their lucid dreaming skills practically. They found that the broad category of having fun drew the most attention from lucid dreamers, with 81.4 percent reporting how they flew around, danced, played games, and so on. The next most common application, at 63.8 percent, involved changing nightmares. Lucid dreamers, especially women, realized that they could use their awareness when lucid to alter a nightmare scenario in some fashion. Schädlich's research showed that problem-solving (29.9 percent), creativity (27.6 percent), and practicing skills (21.3 percent) rounded out the top five applications. Lucid dreamers have thus discovered that all points on the spectrum between outrageous fun and serious work can occur in lucid dreams.[16]

Unfortunately, much of society neglects or devalues dreaming and remains ignorant of lucid dreaming's existence and the scientific evidence for it. Even though a high percentage of the college-age population reports having had a lucid dream experience, few understand the fascinating potential of this unique state. As individuals, science, and society come to understand the potential of lucid dreaming, we feel the number of frequent lucid dreamers will rise even higher.

The Profound Potential of Lucid Dreaming

When people ask us why anyone would want to lucid dream, we immediately suspect they have never had a lucid dream.

For many people, lucid dreaming represents one of the most extraordinary adventures and powerful moments of freedom that they have ever experienced. Often when people become lucid, they report a kind of spontaneous euphoria in which they feel a strong sense of energy and mastery coupled with a profound sense of awareness and clarity. Similar to the self-actualization research done by psychologist Abraham Maslow, many lucid dreamers can point to specific lucid dreams as peak experiences, complete with feelings of wonder, awe, well-being, and expansive awareness.

Yet lucid dreaming has many practical, creative, and profound purposes as well. Following are six reasons to explore lucid dreaming more deeply, with a corresponding lucid dream to illustrate each point.

Freedom and Joy

Many lucid dreamers have reported experiencing a feeling of liberation and joyful freedom while in the lucid dream state. Free of normal physical constraints, you have a broader range of incredible possibilities. Here is how one dreamer described his experience:

> The dream begins at a party in someone's home with lots of people. After a moment, I realize that I do not know these people. This realization prompts me to become lucid. Once lucid, I immediately begin flying through the rooms and laugh as I have fun moving the furniture around with my mind.
>
> Since my flying ability seems excellent, I decide to fly out to the stars. I begin flying very fast upward into the night sky. I find myself flying past planets! Finally, I stop in the weightlessness of space. It's utterly silent. Looking around, I see a planet with a band of rings around it. Then I notice that two of the planet's four moons also have orangeish, gold rings! Joyful, I fly toward the planet's main ring. As I come near the ring, I see it as bits of tiny reflective particles or shiny dust. I move closer and feel touched by tiny bits of

energy on my body, like sparks of energy. I wake from this lucid dream with a feeling of amazement!

In lucid dreaming, the feeling of freedom, wonder and joy seems quite thrilling and spectacular. Initially, you may think: "Oh, it's just a mind game, a playful fantasy." But read on and see how people use lucid dreaming for quite practical purposes and how science can use it to explore the nature of the psyche experimentally.

Inner Creativity

Whatever area of interest you focus on in life, you can use the magic of lucid dreaming to access inner creativity for that specific interest when you are consciously aware. Consider the creativity of regular dreamers reported by Deirdre Barrett in her book *The Committee of Sleep*.[17]

- Paul McCartney: In a dream, he received the tune for the hit "Yesterday."

- Richard Wagner: In a dream, he received the opera *Tristan and Isolde*.

- August Kekule: While dozing off, he dreamed the structure of the benzene molecule, which opened up the field of organic chemistry.

- Otto Loewi: He awakened with an experimental design to explain the chemical transmission of nerve impulses and won the Nobel Prize.

- Dmitri Mendeleev: In a dream, he saw the periodic table of elements.

- Elias Howe: After months of trying to invent a sewing machine, he felt perplexed by how the needle would function, but then had a dream in which he realized a new design for the needle with the eye at the tip. He went on to create the first functional sewing machine.

• William Watt: In recurring dreams in 1782, he saw liquid lead falling from above and landing in water, whereupon it became nice spheres. He experimented with this while awake and created a new way to make gunshot simply and inexpensively.

Google cofounder Larry Page mentions the importance of dreaming in his 2009 commencement address at the University of Michigan. As a twenty-three-year-old doctoral student there, he had a dream. "When I suddenly woke up," he reports, "I was thinking. 'What if we could download the whole web and just keep the links . . . ?' I grabbed a pen and started writing!"[18] He could scarcely imagine how a giant search-engine company would later develop, due in part to this nighttime creativity.

In all these instances, artists, scientists, and inventors used the creativity available to them in dreaming to create beautiful music, solve complex scientific puzzles, invent machinery, and develop amazing new ventures. Now imagine this: What if, in a lucid dream, you could purposefully seek out creativity, answers, and inventions while consciously aware?

Montreal artist Dustyn Lucas reports using lucid dreams to access his inner creativity. Sometimes when lucid dreaming, he asks to see a painting when he steps into a dream gallery or opens a book. In one particular instance, he recalls finding himself in a desert. That struck him as strange, and he realized he must be dreaming. Lucid, he noticed that he had a sketchbook in his hand. Suddenly, he saw an extraordinary image in the sand in front of him and began to make a sketch of it. He writes:

> As I sketched, a person approached from behind and spoke the most perfectly beautiful sentence in the universe; it explained all of existence and, in a dreamlike way, looped back in on itself. I was so excited to have these words that I began to praise the genius of the one that spoke them, when he turned to me and said, "Stop trying to inflate me, just take me full in." Then I awoke; the perfect sentence was gone, but the image in the sand was etched into my memory.[19]

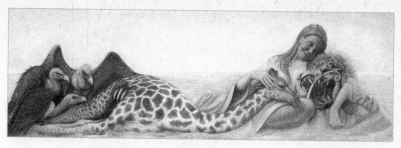

The Mirage of Duality in the Sands of Time, an extraordinary
image revealed to Dustyn Lucas while lucid dreaming.

When I saw Lucas' painting and heard of his accompanying lucid
dream at an International Association for the Study of Dreams (IASD)
conference, I asked him: "What was it like to paint this?" He told me
that it was as if he had painted it before. The process of painting went
considerably faster and easier than a normal painting, since he had
already seen it in his lucid dream. He titled his painting *The Mirage of
Duality in the Sands of Time.*

On Iowa Public Radio, Robert had a show every other month for
about a year and a half. One of these focused on the topic "Dreams,
Lucid Dreams, and Creativity." The switchboard lit up with calls from
people who had experienced dreams that had solved problems for
them or brought them creative gifts.

Among the lucid dreamers who called in to share their stories,
one, a professional rock musician and lyricist, stated that he used lucid
dreaming to seek out and discover new lyrics for songs. Another said he
wrote novels and graduated from the prestigious Iowa Writer's Workshop. He claimed that, when he felt stuck while writing novels, he tried
to have a lucid dream. Once lucid, he called the novel characters to
him and asked: "What is wrong with this novel?" He said they sometimes gave him amazing insights into how to move the novel forward to
completion. You can imagine a novel character telling him in the lucid
dream: "You never should have killed Aunt Sally in chapter 3. We need
her at the end of the book to reveal grandfather's amazing secret!"

An even more practical use for lucid dream creativity comes from
the book *Exploring the World of Lucid Dreaming* by Stephen LaBerge
and Howard Rheingold. They give the example of a software programmer who used lucid dreaming to work out difficult software code. In

this case, once the programmer became lucid, he called for Albert Einstein to join him and work out the code. After they plotted it out in the lucid dream, he sent the dream Einstein away and spent time memorizing the work. Upon waking, he wrote the code out as fast as he could recall it. The lucid dreamer commented: "I take this to work and usually it is 99-percent accurate."[20]

The depth of the unconscious mind in dreams has delighted artists and inventors for millennia and literally changed the world. The advantage of lucid dreaming? You can consciously access your inner muse and deliberately seek assistance from its unfathomable abundance. If you became lucid tonight, what creative issue would you like to experience, resolve, or investigate?

Emotional and Psychological Healing

For twelve years, Robert has co-edited the magazine *Lucid Dreaming Experience* with friend and lucid dreaming colleague, Lucy Gillis. Fans call it the *LDE*. Each issue showcases an interview with an experienced lucid dreamer to see how that person uses lucid dreaming in his or her life.

One interview remains unforgettable. Hope, an airline mechanic, was working on a Boeing 767 when it came loose from its moorings and rolled over her legs, crushing them. The doctors amputated one leg and, for more than six months, she lay in the hospital recovering from her injuries.

Night after night, Hope had a recurring nightmare of being chased. These became "unbearable," and she dreaded falling asleep. Then one day, she discovered a book on lucid dreaming at a bookshop. She remembered having had lucid dreams as a child and the joyful experience of flying consciously. Reading the book, she realized that she could use lucid dreaming to end her nightmares.

Here she tells of the pivotal lucid dream that ended those horrible nightmares:

> The big moment for me was this dream; I was running for my life scared as usual. I knew something was chasing me but I wasn't sure who or what. As I ran and ran, I think that perhaps it occurred to me: *"Hey, I am running but I only*

have one leg." At that moment, I knew I was dreaming, and I got a bit excited.

I realized I was being chased, but suddenly, I was no longer afraid. I stopped running, turned around, and saw the approaching monster. It looked ugly and scary, and he slowed down and realized I had stopped running. As it approached me, I waved at it and smiled a huge smile and then jumped up and flew away. It was so amazing, and I can never forget it. The monster even got a confused look on its face the moment I waved and smiled. As I flew away, I just had fun with flying around. I only had to evade whatever was chasing me and fly away a few more times, and then it was like they realized it was useless to continue to chase me.[21]

Psychologists find these recurring nightmares a common symptom of post-traumatic stress disorder (PTSD). Some therapists have now begun teaching their clients to use lucid dreaming to overcome their recurring nightmares.[22] As in Hope's case, therapists often discover that becoming lucid in one nightmare will severely reduce the frequency of future nightmares or stop them altogether.

Since the publication of Robert's first book, he has received more reports from lucid dreamers who have realized that lucid dreaming may assist them with other issues like overcoming phobias, anxiety, and emotional problems. Others have written to tell how they used lucid dreaming to deal with inner issues like understanding failed relationships so they could move forward in their lives with more energy and joy. Even therapists have told Robert how they used the ideas in his first book to help clients achieve breakthroughs. When you are aware at the level of dreaming, you have a dynamic environment in which to gain insight, practice constructive behaviors, and work through difficult issues.

Physical Healing

Stephen LaBerge conducted a series of experiments that looked at lucidly dreamed actions and their effect on the physical body. He noted that lucid dreaming events—eye movements, changing breathing patterns, tensing muscles—resulted in some degree of a parallel physical event in the body.[23]

Working with the basic concept of using the lucid dream state to affect the physical body and the additional physical healing research using deep hypnosis and visualization, some lucid dreamers have taken the idea further and explored the idea of physical healing in lucid dreams. In this case, provided by Ed Kellogg, you can read a simple, self-reported example of lucid dream healing.[24]

Annie had painful plantar warts on each foot. Every step she took hurt. Nothing seemed to make the plantar warts go away. One day, the teacher of her lucid dreaming group told her of his own successes with healing the physical body while lucid dreaming. He suggested she give it a try in her next lucid dream.

Annie recalls her healing lucid dream: "Something about the light seems strange. I think of my feet because they are hurting me as I walk. So I sit down on a cube, like a wooden cube. Then I remember that I can heal my feet [in a lucid dream]. At that moment, all of the surrounding room drops away to a black void where I sit. I recall using a ball of white light as I had been visualizing [before going to sleep].

Sure enough, the white light appears around my hands. I put my hands on my feet—first, the right one. The light enters the foot and glows golden from within. I hold it there for several seconds and then move to the left foot. Same process. I put both feet down and realize I had done what I had incubated. It seems amazing and terrifying. That feeling is so intense I woke up.

Before this night, Annie could not walk without feeling pain from six plantar warts. In the morning, after the lucid dream, she examined her feet. All the warts had turned black during the night. Within ten days, they all fell off and did not return. She could now walk healed and free of pain.

When you think about this, you realize that the medical establishment could conduct research on lucid dreaming as an alternative healing practice. Imagine research on a group of people with simple, persistent ailments—skin diseases or warts, for example—who are taught to lucid dream, and a control group with the same ailments who are not taught lucid dream healing skills. After a year, which group shows the most improvement? A simple study like this could begin to confirm that healing potential exists in the lucid dream state, and that lucid dreamers can learn successful approaches to accomplish this for themselves.

Lucid dreamer Ed Kellogg has explored the idea of physical healing quite deeply and reports numerous instances of three types of healing assistance appearing in lucid dreams: curative, diagnostic, and prescriptive.[25] In Annie's case, you see a dramatic example of a curative lucid dream, in which the ailment shows significant healing improvement after the dream. In diagnostic lucid dreams, dreamers gather information about the nature of an ailment or impending ailment, because sometimes they or the medical establishment feels uncertain about the actual source of their symptoms. Finally, in prescriptive lucid dreams, dreamers learn about specific items that may encourage healing—a specific medicine, diet, practice, or other prescriptive aid literally or symbolically shown in the dream.

Lucid dreamers have considered the concept of physical healing for a few decades. In 1987, researchers Stephen LaBerge and Jayne Gackenbach created a survey of lucid dreamers for *OMNI* magazine that asked whether the subjects had used lucid dreaming for physical healing. They received a number of apparently valid self-reports of physical healing in lucid dreams.[26] In her article "The Potential of Lucid Dreaming for Bodily Healing," Gackenbach notes:

> Ailments represented included a recurring headache, menstrual cramps and hives, sprained ankle, pulled muscle, torn ligament and skin cancer. It is important to keep in mind that none of the cures reported by the *OMNI* readers can be called miraculous, but they may demonstrate that during the enhanced state of mental imagery called dreams one can intuit and perhaps affect the health of one's body. At the least, certain commonalties can be found among these examples that hint at a pattern of apparent dream healing.[27]

LaBerge's work on the psychophysical relations of lucid dreaming actions to body processes and Kellogg's exploration of numerous cases of physical healing after lucid dreams show both the conceptual and practical potential of this approach. Although individuals continue to report new successes, the world of medicine has basically ignored this exciting area of treatment, touched on by LaBerge and Gackenbach almost three decades ago.

Psychological Insight

In *Nightlight: The Lucidity Institute Newsletter*, a lucid dreamer identified as A. T. reported on a life-changing lucid dream epiphany about the importance of belief. In her dream, she rented a pair of wings for twenty-five cents and used them to fly around the dream easily.[28] Then she thought: "It was ridiculous that a pair of cheap rented wings could sustain me." With that thought, she began plummeting to the earth!

This battle between first believing in the power of the wings and then not believing eventually made her become lucid. She realized she was dreaming, and that "it was my belief that I could fly that enabled me to fly—not any artificial devices or other means of external support." After this lesson in lucidity, she realized the importance of belief in her lucid dreams.

The next week, in waking life, A. T. interviewed for a job. During the interview, she felt about ready to give up, but then recalled the lucid dream and the importance of having self-confident beliefs. With that realization, she says: "I found myself saying positive things about my resourcefulness and commitment to hard work." Guess what? She got the job.

Some lucid dreamers call transferring lessons from the lucid dream realm to waking reality an example of living lucidly. Many of us have powerful stories of becoming more lucid about our current thinking and expectations, which suddenly worked to change our waking life situations for the better. Lucid dreaming may show you exactly how you can work with the unconscious to improve your life situation. Often, lucid dreams show you areas of self-limiting beliefs and doubts, which you may need to resolve to move forward with your personal development.

German psychologist Paul Tholey deeply explored lucid dreaming after teaching himself how to become lucid in 1959 as a college student. Later, he did some of the first work on using lucid dreams as an inner platform to improve athletes' skill levels.[29] He taught skiers and snowboarders to lucid dream and then encouraged them to practice their sports in the lucid dream state. In fact, he suggested that they try to push their skills to the limit and attain new sensory-motor abilities in the dream, knowing it as a lucid dream where they could not be physically hurt. The waking-world result? Tholey felt most showed considerable improvement in their athletic ability and competitiveness.

Researchers Daniel Erlacher and Michael Schredl have sought to replicate Tholey's findings on sports practice by having lucid dreamers perform a simple game in which they toss a coin into a cup two meters away while lucid, and then again when awake. After completing this task in a lucid dream, their waking performance improved. The researchers note: "[T]he results of this study showed that rehearsing in a lucid dream enhances subsequent performance in wakefulness."[30]

Spirituality and Wisdom

In many wisdom traditions, the practice of lucid dreaming can be used for spiritual insight and growth. For example, 11th-century Buddhist yogi Naropa called dream yoga (which relies on lucid dreaming as a main technique) one of the six paths to enlightenment. According to many teachers of Tibetan Buddhist traditions, lucid dreaming can educate you in the true nature of the mind and help bring greater awareness to your experience so that you can see through your habitual reactions and your connection to mental phenomena. With practice, lucid dreaming can possibly serve to lead you to an experience of non-duality, a special state of awareness in which no subject/object duality exists.

Tenzin Wangyal Rinpoche, a lama in the Tibetan Buddhist tradition, explains: "If one fully accomplishes dream yoga, one is prepared to enter the intermediate state after death with the correct view and the stability in non-dual presence needed to attain liberation."[31] In essence, lucid dreaming serves as a supportive practice in clarifying the mind, breaking reactive mental connections, and helping the student move beyond *samsara*, the cyclic existence of rebirth.

You can also encounter lucid dreaming's spiritual potential in the works of other wisdom traditions—notably Sufism, Taoism, Hinduism, and many native shamanic traditions. In each case, lucid dreaming receives serious consideration as a powerful path for spiritual insight, understanding, and personal growth.

Of course, a person does not need to align with any tradition to experiment with spiritual practices in the lucid dream state. Here's my personal example of using the practice of meditation to empty the mind into a lucid dream:

> Walking along a trail, it suddenly strikes me as being too strange, and I realize I am dreaming. I think about what to do and remember a friend asked me if I had ever tried meditating in a lucid dream. Thinking about this, I stop on the trail and sit down in a half lotus position. With my eyes open, I begin meditating.
>
> I begin to quiet my mind. Suddenly, the dream scene in front of me begins to be ripped open in places, and brilliant white light shoots through the holes! After more and more of the dream scene disappears, I stop for a moment in the light. Then I decide: "Perhaps, I should close my eyes." Now with eyes closed, I begin meditating again and within seconds, I experience an extraordinary clarity of awareness, profound sense of ego-less enlargement, and feeling of transcendental Oneness.

So when someone asks you why you bother to lucid dream, you can describe the incredibly profound possibilities accessible when dreaming lucidly: joyful freedom, creativity, emotional healing, physical healing, psychological insights, and spiritual growth.

Chapter 2

PREPARING TO DREAM LUCIDLY

Strong dream recall has a positive correlation with lucid dreaming.[32] When you recall more dreams, it suggests that your awareness and memory of dreaming have increased. Moreover, remembering more dreams increases the chance of remembering your lucid dreams. So let's briefly take a look at a wide range of preparatory practices that can enhance your success with lucid dreaming.

Virtually everyone has five or more dreams each night. Daily, we spend about two hours dreaming, or almost 9 percent of each day. This means that for every eleven years of your life, you spend one of them completely in a dream state. Yet almost every time I give a workshop, someone raises a hand and says: "What if you do not remember your dreams?"

At a presentation in Colorado, a young man asked me that same question. I offered two main reasons why most people do not recall their dreams. First, they feel that dreams have no value and therefore do not warrant being remembered. Second, they have become frightened of dreams and decide not to recall them.

This young man told me that he was twenty-six years old and had not had a dream in ten years. I asked: "What happened to you ten years ago at age sixteen?" He looked puzzled for a moment and then realized: "Oh, my parents had a horrible divorce." I told him that sometimes we consciously or unconsciously decide *not to remember our dreams*. However, tonight before sleep, he could tell his inner awareness that he was now ready to remember them. The next morning, he joyfully ran up to me in the conference room and said:

Before sleep, I told my inner awareness that I was ready to remember my dreams. Then as I began to fall asleep, I saw dream images, like a slide show of dream images, one after the other! It felt as if this happened all night. I am so happy that I can dream.

Of course, he did have dreams during those previous ten years; he simply had to allow them to be seen.

Improving your dream recall seems a valuable practice for those who want to dream lucidly. Ideally, you should be able to recall at least one dream a night, if not more, before beginning the lucid dream practices in this book.

If you do not have strong recall, try suggesting to yourself before sleep: "I will find it easy to recall my dreams when I wake." If you wish, you can suggest to yourself that you wake up after each dream. If that seems too much, then you can suggest before sleep that you will recall the most important dream of the night.

In rare instances, a third reason may exist for poor dream recall—a prescribed medication or a physical condition like sleep apnea, for example. At a bookstore talk in Ann Arbor, Michigan, an attendee noted that certain conditions like sleep apnea (in which a person pauses in breathing or has very shallow breathing) can negatively affect dream recall. Also, some widely prescribed medications can negatively affect it, which a careful reading of the medication's possible side effects should show. If you have a medical condition, seek competent medical guidance.

Dream Recall

To succeed at lucid dreaming, your first thought upon waking should be the question: "What was I just dreaming?" You should instinctively reach for your pen (or voice recorder) to make some nocturnal notes about your most recent dream while it remains fresh in your mind. Some people tell me that they drink an extra glass of water before going to sleep, just so that they will have to wake up in the middle of the night. When they do wake up, they first think to recall their last dream. Later, as they go back to sleep, they fix their intention to become lucid in the next dream.

How to Recall Dreams

- Keep a dream journal and a pen, pencil, or voice-activated recorder by your bed.

- Develop the habit of immediately asking yourself each time you awaken at night: "What was I just dreaming?" Focus on recalling the dream.

- Quietly make a few notes in your journal each time you wake. Jot down a few keywords (for example, "dinosaur," "library") that will help you recall the dream in the morning.

- Write down your dreams in the morning, even if only as dream fragments. At the top of each entry, put the date.

- Give yourself enough time for sleeping. As the night progresses, your dreams get longer and longer, which increases your chance of becoming lucid.

- Have fun with it. Realize when a dream gives you clues to help you become lucidly aware. See how close you can get to lucidity.

Some research has shown that certain B vitamins and folic acid may help with overall memory performance. So before sleep, some people take a B vitamin (specifically B12, B6, and folic acid) or introduce natural foods with those vitamins into their normal diet.[33] Try this for a short time and notice the effect. Do your dreams seem clearer? More vivid? More memorable? Do you feel more aware while dreaming?

Some people have developed habits that reduce dream recall. For example, they sleep next to their mobile phones and frequently wake to check out the latest text or email. Or worse, they let the phone ring and beep at night, which interferes with regular sleep and dreaming. After some time with this habit, their first thought upon waking involves checking their messages. As a result, they tend to develop poor dream recall.

Other obstructive habits involve taking substances that inhibit dreaming or dream recall—alcohol (which reduces REM time)[34] and certain drugs, for example. If you are uncertain about how your evening activities affect your dreaming, try changing your evening habits for a few days and see what happens to your dream recall.

Levels of Lucid Dreaming

Many people think of lucid dreaming as black and white—you either have a lucid dream or you don't. With experience, you discover that there are various levels of lucid dreaming. Ed Kellogg created a Lucidity Continuum to show the progression of these levels of awareness in his experience.[35] A simplified and edited version follows, but for those interested, the entire Continuum with additional levels can be seen at *www.improverse.com/ed-articles/kellogg*.

It may help to think of the levels of lucid dreaming awareness as being like the dimmer switch on a light panel. At the lowest level, the light barely functions and the change in awareness seems very dim or slight. As you move the dimmer switch higher, however, your lucid awareness (the light) increases. At full power, you have achieved full lucidity and feel a strong awareness. Consider these ascending levels of lucid awareness.

Pre-lucid: You notice some sort of bizarreness and find it unusual for waking physical reality. For example, you write in your dream journal: "My horse had six legs. This struck me as very strange as I cinched the saddle."

Sub-lucid: You have a vague realization that you dream, but do not understand what that means or act on the implications. In your dream journal, you may write: "My sister, Mary, attended my son's graduation party. I remembered that this seems impossible because she lives in Tokyo. I wondered whether I dreamed this, but decided to take care of the party guests."

Semi-lucid: You realize that you are dreaming but, for the most part, go along with it and make few adjustments. Your dream journal may read: "I saw my Aunt Maria but remembered she died three years ago. My mom told me to prepare the guest bed for her, so I did. But I used dream magic to do so because I realized I dreamed it."

Lucid: You realize completely that you are dreaming and act to make major choices and decisions in the dream. An example from a dream journal may read: "When I saw my childhood house in Miami, I knew it no longer existed. That thought made me realize I was dreaming. So I decided to grab my dog and go flying. We flew above the city and past the marina. I saw something interesting on a beach and flew over to investigate."

Fully lucid: You realize you are dreaming, feel a considerable degree of mastery, and can easily recall experiments that you wished to perform. You may write in your dream journal: "Now lucid, I thought, 'What experiment did Michael and I discuss yesterday? Oh, he asked me to see whether I could get over my fear of heights by going to the top of a high building in my lucid dream and looking over the edge.' So I looked around and saw a very high building and decided that since I could not be hurt, I would go to the very top and practice looking over the edge."

Super lucid: You feel a very high degree of personal energy, clarity of thought, memory, creativity, and dream manipulation. Your dream report may say: "As we fall through the wall, I know I dream. I feel very energetic and sharp and decide to soar into the night sky. After flying, I stop and recall my plan. I decide to practice meditating in a lucid dream. As I focus inward, suddenly, the lucid dream scene changes and I find myself . . ."

When you read lucid dream reports, you will notice various levels of awareness. In fact, these levels fluctuate even within one dream, because your lucid awareness can increase or decrease according to your actions and focus. Later, you will learn tips on how to hold on to your lucid awareness and stay securely in your lucid dreams.

Common Lucid Dreams and Their Lessons

In my early years of lucid dreaming, I quickly learned one important point: *Every lucid dream has a lesson for the dreamer.* If you examine your lucid dreams closely, you will learn important lessons that teach you how to become lucid, how to stay lucid longer, and how to succeed in manipulating your dreams.

Let's look at some common lucid dreams that beginners have reported and see what lessons they hold.

Dream 1: I saw my childhood friend and realized I was dreaming because I knew she lived far away in Berlin. Seeing her again, I became so excited and filled with emotion that, suddenly, the lucid dream ended.

> *Lesson*: The lucid dream state has rules. Some dreamers discover that if they feel extremely excited, their lucid dreams become unstable and collapse, so they learn to modulate their emotions within a certain range and keep the dream stable. As a lucid dreamer, always consider what happens immediately before a lucid dream suddenly ends. If you notice what precedes the dream's collapse, you can use that knowledge to avoid it in the future.

Dream 2: After finding myself in the jungle, I couldn't recall how I had gotten there. Then I realized that I must be dreaming. I began to explore. I noticed an amazing butterfly about two feet long. I had never seen one like this before and kept staring at it. The lucid dream became unstable and seemed kind of shaky. Suddenly, it ended, and I woke up.

> *Lesson*: Here, the dreamer stared fixedly at an object for too long and the dream collapsed. Around the world, lucid dreamers have learned to avoid staring rigidly at things. After about five seconds of fixed staring, many have discovered that their lucid dreams collapse. So do not stare. Instead, make a habit of turning away every now and then or lightly looking at captivating images.

Dream 3: I was walking in the park and noticed that my steps were very long, like two meters! This made me think: "I am dreaming." I walked around and talked to dream figures. Then I saw a man who played a flute for a dancing snake. I found this interesting. I watched him play his flute. I even forgot I was dreaming this. The snake began to move toward me, and I got worried and ran away!

> *Lesson*: Awareness can fluctuate markedly. You can lose lucid awareness through a lack of attention and critical awareness. If you allow yourself to become captivated by dream events, you may lose your lucid awareness completely and silently slip into regular dreaming.

Dream 4: In my dreams, when I begin to do things that are inappropriate or wrong, suddenly my mom appears. She just stares at me and makes me feel really uncomfortable. Even though I know I'm dreaming and try to get rid of her, she won't leave. Do you know why or have any suggestions? Thanks!" (Submitted by a lucid dreamer, Jason, to my first book's website.)

> *Lesson*: Even though Jason has gained lucid awareness, the unexpected appearance of his mother illustrates that the lucid dreamer does not completely control the lucid dream. The lucid dreamer may find that feelings, thoughts and latent beliefs (in this case, guilt and worry) spontaneously call forth corresponding dream objects or figures. Here, the dream figure of the disapproving mom suggests that the lucid dreamer needs to make some type of inner changes, such as resolving his guilt.

Dream 5: I saw a clock moving backward and thought: "This is a dream!" Then I remembered that I heard on the radio a lucid dreaming expert say: "In a lucid dream, gravity does not exist." Suddenly, I floated up to the ceiling and could not get down!

> *Lesson*: Your belief system influences your actions and your relationship to the dream. If you believe in gravity, then

your belief in it makes it active in your dream experience. If you change your mind and decide not to believe in gravity, then you will not be affected by it in the lucid dream.

Dream 6: While lucid, I began flying through the air by swimming with my hands. I went higher and higher. Then I looked at the ground and became concerned by the height. I started to drop and fell to the ground!

> *Lesson*: Your lucid dream usually reflects your belief system at that time. Your thoughts can expand or limit your actions in a lucid dream. Therefore, pay attention to your beliefs. If you believe that physical action (e.g., swimming with your hands) will help you move, it will. And if you believe that you are in danger of falling and focus on that possibility, you activate that potential. To succeed at lucid dreaming requires adopting a broader and more flexible set of beliefs that see lucid dreaming as a mental environment with largely mental rules.

Dream 7: Aware in a lucid dream, I decide to talk to a dream figure. I ask him: "Do you know I am dreaming you?" He responds: "How do you know I am not dreaming you?" I reply: "Well look, I can fly." And I begin to fly. He says: "Well look, I can fly, too." And he flies too. I felt very confused.

> *Lesson*: As you see in this actual example, unexpected things can happen in a lucid dream. Dream figures, for example, can seem more aware than the lucid dreamer and do completely surprising things—like question you. This should help you realize and accept that even more exists in lucid dreams than your expectations and mental models.

How to Identify Lessons

Assuming you have a lucid dream, write it out. Can you identify two lessons you learned from it? Look closely and consider what lessons in lucidity were there for you, and how this may assist you in future lucid dreams.

My father served as a pilot. After each flight mission, he had a debriefing; the commanding officer wanted to know how the flight crew had performed, what areas needed improvement, and so on. So make a habit of having your own, personal lucid dream debriefing to see what lessons you have learned and how you can improve.

Ask yourself questions like these after each lucid dream:

- How did I become lucid?

- Did I do anything special the day before that may have assisted my becoming lucid (e.g., put new sheets on the bed, worked hard outside in the sun, read lucid dreams before sleep)?

- What went smoothly in the lucid dream?

- What unexpected things happened?

- How did I handle unusual events?

- What other responses could I have made?

- How did the lucid dream end?

- How could I have prolonged the lucid dream?

By thinking deeply about your lucid dreams, you can discover the important lessons that you need to learn to make them longer, more stable, and more satisfying. In addition, significant patterns may appear that help you understand what actions or changes increase your chance for becoming lucidly aware.

Lucid Dreaming: Influence or Control?

Lucid dreamers do not control their lucid dreams. When you read most lucid dreams carefully, they show that lucid dreamers rather *influence* their dreams. Although they may control their personal actions and focus, just as in waking life, they do not control the dreams—any more than you control waking life or the highway on which you drive. In the section above, you saw examples of lucid dreamers influencing and manipulating their dreams, but none of them completely controlled their dreams.

Consider Dream 4, in which the disapproving mother appears when the dreamer does something inappropriate. If he controls the dream, why does she appear? It seems obvious that the dreamer directs his personal actions within the dream, but does not control the entire dream process.

Or consider a lucid dreamer who flies through a wall and discovers a beautiful beach and sailboat on the other side. Who created that beach and sailboat? The dreamer did not consciously create it or decide for it to appear there, he just simply flew through the wall and found it there. Obviously, dreamers experience and influence many things, but do not control every facet of the lucid dreaming experience. In my first book, I use the analogy cited earlier by Caroline: "No sailor controls the sea."[36] Like sailors on the sea, we merely direct our perceptual awareness within the larger state of dreaming.

Some of the problems arising around the idea of control seem attributable to what scientists call "confirmation bias," or the tendency to focus on information that confirms our preconceptions and beliefs. In this case, when dreamers believe that lucid dreaming means control of the dream, they point to occasions when they appear to control it, while completely ignoring the many unexpected actions and uncontrolled events that occur in their dreams. Confirmation bias can often blind us to a proper understanding of the actual nature of lucid dreaming.

So please keep this in mind: Lucid dreamers influence their dreams and guide their own activities, but do not completely control their dreams. This idea may seem like an academic point now; however, understanding this becomes crucially important as you go deeper into lucid dreaming.

How to Score Your Lucidity

Setting goals can make a simple task seem more amusing and rewarding. Here's how you can use Kellogg's Lucidity Continuum to motivate your awareness for success with lucid dreaming.

1. Think of something that motivates you—a special treat, a drink, a food, or some event (like going to a movie) that you can use to reward yourself. Write down some motivators.

2. Give point values to each level of lucidity: one point for having a pre-lucid dream, two for having a sub-lucid dream, three for a semi-lucid dream, four for a lucid dream, five for a fully lucid dream, and six for a super-lucid dream. (If you have a hard time recalling dreams, then give yourself one point for recalling three dreams in one night!)

3. Think about your current level of dreaming and lucid dreaming. How many lucid dreaming points did you achieve in the past week? If none of your dreams met the criteria for a pre-lucid dream or higher, your score is zero. If you had one lucid dream (four points) and one sub-lucid dream (two points), your score is six.

4. Set a point goal for the coming week and use your motivational item as a reward for meeting or exceeding that goal. Whatever point goal you choose, make sure it stretches your talents.

However you play the game, have fun with it! Each morning, carefully review your dream journal and watch your lucid dreaming points increase. See whether you can out-perform your previous week or month. If it matters to you, then you will consciously reinforce that desired behavior.

Chapter 3

BASIC INDUCTION TECHNIQUES

Hundreds of thousands of people have used simple lucid dreaming techniques to become consciously aware in dreams. Although this book provides a number of techniques for inducing lucid dreams, we strongly encourage you to try one technique for an entire month to learn that specific technique fully. Please do not hop from one technique to another.

As you sample the various techniques, you may find that some appeal to you more than others. Certain techniques rely on suggestion, while others involve creating or re-creating convincing dream visualizations. A few ask you to change daytime thought patterns, so that the new thoughts and questions will appear in your dreams and prompt lucidity (based on the continuity theory in which dream content often seems to follow waking interests and emotional preoccupations). Whichever technique you select, please practice it faithfully to achieve the best results.

Let's start with the first technique I used to become lucidly aware: the modified Castaneda technique of finding your hands.

Finding Your Hands

In 1975, I read Carlos Castaneda's book, *Journey to Ixtlan*. Castaneda was a UCLA graduate student in anthropology studying psychoactive plants. He decided to seek out a traditional native teacher and met a Yaqui shaman, whom he called don Juan. Don Juan began to teach Castaneda to question traditional Western assumptions and to practice new ways of looking at experienced reality. Castaneda became don Juan's apprentice and learned these new practices.

In *Journey to Ixtlan*, don Juan suggests that Castaneda do something simple to become consciously aware in the dream state: "Tonight in your dreams," he instructs, "you must look at your hands." When Castaneda protests that it sounds impossible, don Juan tells him: "Imagine all the inconceivable things you could accomplish [when aware in your dreams] . . . but pick one thing in advance and find it in your dreams. I said your hands because they'll always be there."[37]

Because I was a junior in high school when I read this book and was very curious, I wondered whether I could actually accomplish the task of finding my hands in a dream. Don Juan's suggestions on how to do this boiled down to simply trying to do it. I used his hints and my own youthful knowledge about the power of suggestion to create the modified Castaneda technique of finding your hands. After three nights of using it, I had my first deliberately induced lucid dream. Over time, I perfected the technique into a simple practice.

How to Find Your Hands in a Dream

Here is my modified version of the Castaneda technique:

- Sit in your bed and become mentally settled.

- Look softly at the palms of your hands and tell yourself in a relaxed manner: "Tonight while I am dreaming, I will see my hands and realize that I am dreaming."

- Continue to look softly at your hands and mentally repeat: "Tonight while I am dreaming, I will see my hands and realize that I am dreaming."

- Allow your eyes to become unfocused or to cross, if they naturally do so. Remain at peace and continue to repeat the suggestion slowly. Allow your mind to go blank as you look at your hands and repeat the suggestion.

- After about five minutes, or if you are too sleepy, quietly end the practice.

- When you wake up in the middle of the night, gently recall your intention to see your hands. Did you dream of seeing your hands?

- At some point in a dream, your hands may suddenly appear, and you will instantly make the connection: "My hands. This is a dream!" Your hands may pop up in front of you, or you may notice them as you open a door or climb a ladder. When you see them and realize that you are dreaming, remain calm and lucidly explore the dream environment.

I did this practice faithfully for three successive nights. On the third night, I found myself walking in my high school hallway when suddenly my hands popped up in front of my face! I thought: "My hands. This is a dream!" To realize that I had become consciously aware within dreaming completely amazed me. Things felt real and looked real, even though I knew that I dreamed them. My first actively sought lucid dream became an amazing adventure!

Since that time, many people have told me about their experiences with finding their hands. Some said they saw their hands as they reached to open a strange door or climb a ladder and then thought: "My hands! This is a dream." Others said they saw them, but realized they had far too many fingers; this made them lucid. One person even told me that his hands popped up right in front of him and began to slap him gently on his face until he became lucid. And, finally, a woman in California told me that she looked at her hands before going to sleep. Her husband asked her about the practice, and she explained it. *That night in his dreams, his hands suddenly appeared before him, and he became lucid.*

I believe this Castaneda technique works by mentally establishing a simple stimulus/response associational link, like Ivan Pavlov discovered in his psychophysiological work on conditioned responses in dogs.

Pavlov rang a bell every time he fed his dogs. After pairing the ringing of the bell with the presentation of food, the dogs responded automatically to the ringing of the bell (i.e., they salivated). In my case, seeing my hands automatically called forth the thought: "This is a dream!"

Research in behavioral psychology teaches us that repeatedly practicing a technique strengthens the associational link between the stimulus (the sight of your hands) and the mental response ("This is a dream!"). Thus for best results, you must practice this consistently every night before sleep. Also, you may want to take fifteen seconds during the day and simply look at your hands while repeating: "Tonight while I am dreaming, I will see my hands and realize that I am dreaming."

After many months, I noticed that the technique worked best when I could completely disengage my thought process or empty my mind, if only for an instant. In the Castaneda tradition, this involved the ceasing of internal dialogue. Even though I repeated the suggestion over and over, suddenly, it seemed as if part of me disengaged from all of that and entered a peaceful stillness or emptiness. Although the outer portion of me repeated the suggestion, an inner portion of me became utterly still. On those nights, I noticed that I frequently became lucid. So you can approach this simple technique with the deeper goal of shutting off the internal dialogue of your thought process while looking at your hands.

One reason that some people like this approach is that they can use it before sleep. They do not need to do anything in the middle of the night other than recall their last dream. As a result, they perform the practice before sleep and then wait for the magic to happen.

The Power of Suggestion

A very common and simple technique for inducing lucid dreams involves active mental suggestion before sleep. At its heart, suggestion activates an inner allowance or an inner acceptance of your expressed intent. The famous hypnotherapist Milton Erickson reminds us of a powerful idea when he says: "The unconscious is always listening." Use the power of suggestion to allow yourself access and entry to the wonders of lucid dreaming.

As a preparatory practice, first seek to clear your mind. You may imagine the entire day pictured before you as a drawing on a chalkboard. Now grab the eraser and begin to erase it. Erase all the day's residue. Relax.

Before sleep, repeat to yourself one of the following suggestions for four or five minutes. Flood your mind with the suggestion so that it remains your only prominent intent before falling asleep:

- "Tonight in my dreams, I will realize I am dreaming and become consciously aware."

- "Tonight in my dreams, I will be more critically aware, and when I experience something odd, I will realize I am dreaming and become lucid."

- "Tonight in my dreams, some part of me will stay aware and then inform me when I am dreaming, so I will realize I am dreaming" (e.g., the part of you that wakes you up exactly at 4 a.m. to catch an early airplane flight, even before your alarm clock rings a minute later).

When using suggestion, it helps to visualize and feel your success. After using these suggestions before sleep, imagine yourself happily writing down your lucid dream in the morning. Feel the success as if you have already achieved your goal. Allow the suggestion and your sense of success to pervade your thinking.

If you wish, you can play around with the wording of the suggestion. Some people feel too pushy using the verb *will* and prefer to change it to *allow*, as in: "Tonight in my dreams, I allow myself to be more critically aware, and when I experience something odd, I allow myself to realize I am dreaming and become lucid." Play with the wording until you feel comfortable and pleased with it.

How to Use Mental Suggestion

Write down the three suggestions given above. Circle one suggestion that appeals to you and write it at the top of your dream journal.

Take a moment to memorize the precise wording of it. Then flood your mind with the suggestion before falling asleep. Make it your primary intent and focus as you fall asleep.

Hypnosis and Lucid Dreaming

A few research studies use hypnosis to encourage lucid dreaming. Dr. Joseph Dane researched this in the 1980s, using college students at the University of Virginia who had shown responsiveness to hypnotic induction.[38] These students had no previous experience with lucid dreaming, however.

With one group, Dane used the hypnotic suggestion: "Tonight, you're going to turn off the automatic pilot in your dreams and fly with awareness. Tonight as you dream, you will somehow manage to recognize that you are dreaming while you're dreaming. Something will happen in your dreams to trigger your awareness, and you will remember that you are dreaming."

To another group, Dane suggested that they discover a personal dream symbol in the night's dreaming to aid them in becoming lucid. He reports that one young woman dreamed of a powerful woman in a cape on that night. The next night, the young woman saw the same powerful woman again and suddenly realized that she must be dreaming.

Dane's research study found that those who discovered a personal dream symbol to prompt lucidity had especially powerful lucid dreams. "The qualitative level of their experience," he concluded, "was well beyond what would normally be expected in laboratory experiments."[39] Those with a personal dream symbol had longer and more interesting lucid dreams when compared to those without one.

Overall, Dane's study showed that most became lucid within a few nights when subjected to hypnotic suggestion. This seems very positive for those lucid dreamers who respond positively to hypnosis or self-hypnosis.

Already, some lucid dream hypnosis applications exist. However, please take care to investigate the hypnotic induction used. For example, one oft-used hypnotic suggestion—"You are now walking down a long stairway. With each step, you go deeper into relaxation."—may seem fine in the waking state. However, in your dream state, walking down a long stairway may feel symbolically charged and possibly even a bit scary. Seek out dream-neutral imagery for hypnotic induction.

Dreamsigns

In *Exploring the World of Lucid Dreaming*, Stephen LaBerge coins the term *dreamsigns* to indicate those out-of-place features in a dream that may signal that we are dreaming.[40] The unusual nature of dreamsigns often prompts lucid dreamers to realize that they are dreaming.

LaBerge identifies four general types of dreamsigns that may elicit lucidity and cause you to think: "This is a dream!"

> **Inner Awareness:** You have a peculiar thought, a strong emotion, feel an unusual sensation, or have altered perceptions. For example, you realize that the quality of light seems strange and then realize this must be a dream.
>
> **Action:** You, another dream character, or a dream object does something unusual or impossible in waking life. For example, you go flying and realize this only happens in dreams.
>
> **Form:** Your shape, the shape of a dream character, or that of a dream object appears oddly formed, deformed, or transforming. For example, as you watch, your mother appears as a small girl, then as a teenager, then as her current age, which strikes you as strange, and you realize it must be a dream.
>
> **Context:** The place or situation in a dream seems too unusual. For example, you find yourself at a party talking with a British prince and his wife and wonder how you got invited. Then it hits you: "This must be a dream!"

If you have already had lucid dreams, identify a dreamsign (or dreamsigns) that prompted you to become lucid and write it down. For example, instead of walking down the stairs, you floated down them and realized: "This is a dream."

Although LaBerge suggests that you can pick a dreamsign from your dream journal, I feel few people select something that will honestly activate their critical awareness. Instead, you can ask your dreams for a dreamsign that will work specifically for you. At weekend workshops, almost all of the participants find a significant dreamsign on the first night.

How to Request a Dreamsign

- On a night when you feel ready, sincerely request a dream that will provide you with a clear dreamsign to help you become lucidly aware. Request that you will immediately grasp the dreamsign and recognize it as such in the morning. By using this incubated request, the dreamsign comes as an offering of your inner awareness.

- After you make your special request, write down what dreamsign appears. Remember that a dreamsign may involve context, form, action, or inner awareness. Yours may come as a sensation, an impossible event, a transformation, or something else.

- Determine exactly how the dreamsign prompts your critical awareness. For example, if you see a floating giraffe in your dream, what aspect of that scene prompts your awareness that you dream? The giraffe? Or the fact that an animal floats?

- Encourage your personal dreamsign through suggestion before sleep. In the preceding example, you may say: "Tonight in my dreams, when I see animals floating, I will realize I am dreaming and become lucidly aware."

The Light at Your Throat

One ancient dreamsign that many have used involves the pre-sleep visualization of a candle or special light at the base of the throat. In this practice, you imagine that a lit candle or light representing the light of awareness emerges from the base of your throat. Focus on this visualization as you go to sleep, with the intent that the light of awareness will carry over into your sleeping consciousness and activate lucid awareness. Visualize the candle clearly in your mind.

Some Buddhist traditions teach a variation of this using special imagery.[41] In general, these traditions ask you to visualize that a red lotus sits at the base of your throat, and a white light emerges from its center. The white light may come in the shape of a clear white AH symbol (or A, ཨ) in the middle of the lotus. Clearly see the red lotus with a white glowing AH (or A) symbol as you go to sleep. Continue to focus on this visualization as you go to sleep, with the intent to become lucid.

I have used this basic technique successfully and felt awed to see the candle-like flame emerging from my throat while dreaming. As soon as I saw the lit candle at my throat, I realized that I was dreaming. It seemed a fascinating, yet ancient, way to become consciously aware.

Five Common Questions from Beginners

Since many dreamers have similar experiences when they begin to dream lucidly, they often ask the same questions about their experiences. Here are some of the most common questions asked by beginners:

When am I most likely to have a lucid dream?

Lucid dreams can occur at any time during sleep. However, most people report lucid dreams in the night's final two dream periods or REM cycles. The Lucidity Institute's newsletter, *NightLight*, stated that the average time for lucid dreaming occurs basically six and a half hours after falling asleep for those who sleep in a single seven-to-eight-hour sleep period.

In the morning after a lucid dream, will I feel tired?

No. Normally when you awake after a lucid dream, you feel wonderfully energized and have a lucid afterglow or sense of contentment that stays with you for many hours.

Will lucid dreaming harm my normal dreaming?

No. Most people interested in lucid dreaming find it assists dreaming, because they recall many more dreams. Also, most lucid dreamers discover that lucid dreams account for 5 percent or less of their dreams (30 nights x 5 dreams = 150 dreams a month). So even a talented lucid dreamer may have only seven or eight lucid dreams a month. When looked at in this way, more than 95 percent of your dreams will continue in their usual fashion.

Which technique should I try?

Choose a technique that appeals to you and use it for the month. I suggest the finding-your-hands technique as a place to begin because everyone can do this before sleep, intending to become lucid. It only requires a bit of thought in the middle of the night. You simply wait for your hands to appear, and immediately respond: "My hands! This must be a dream."

What constitutes a reality check?

A reality check is a convincing action you can perform that helps establish that you are dreaming. For example, you may want to see whether you can levitate. If you can, this proves you are dreaming. Other examples include pulling on your finger to see whether it grows longer or putting your hand through a wall or table. Some try to read the same paragraph twice without the words changing, because if the words change, it indicates you are dreaming. Some hold their nose closed to see if they need to breathe; if not, then you are dreaming. If you feel uncertain about the results, you may have to do a couple of reality checks.

Inducing Lucid Dreams

Broadly speaking, you could say that three gateways exist for encouraging and inducing lucid dreams: the mental, the biochemical, and the electromagnetic. Most lucid dream techniques use the mental gateway. Actions, like suggestion, hypnosis, memory triggers, critical questioning, and creating lucid dreamsigns, primarily rely on changing your mind and thought process to recognize, remember, and respond to your intent or subtle dream prompts. With the proper focus and practice, this mental gateway can often lead to consistent lucid dreams.

The biochemical gateway to encouraging lucid dreams varies in its approaches. On the one hand, a person may use vitamins, supplements, or a certain diet to promote a vibrant memory and cognitive function. For some, this may be as simple as drinking a small bit of coffee before sleep with the idea that a tiny dose of caffeine may enhance dream awareness. On the other hand, a person may alter routine sleep/wake patterns to take advantage of rhythmic changes in body chemistry or consciousness, and thereby increase the chance of becoming lucidly aware.

The electromagnetic gateway to encouraging lucid dreams seems a bit more technological, though a May 2014 study in *Nature Neuroscience* sounds intriguing. A team of researchers led by Ursula Voss worked with twenty-seven subjects who were inexperienced lucid dreamers. In the sleep lab, they outfitted the subjects with electrodes strategically placed on areas of the scalp above the fronto-temporal brain. When the subjects entered REM sleep (dreaming), the researchers activated the four transcranial alternating current stimulation electrodes at various frequencies. As stimulation frequencies entered the gamma band of 25 to 40 hz, they discovered that the majority of the subjects reported becoming lucidly aware in the dream (if only for a few moments). Additional research and replication of this study seems appropriate, but it may lead to a very exciting new era in lucid dream induction.[42]

Other electrical devices have assisted some in becoming lucidly aware. Most notably, certain sleep masks have been marketed that monitor your dream cycles and then provide a flashing light or auditory cue to incite lucidity. Hopefully, the flashing light or auditory cue will enter the dream and cause you to think, "A flashing light? This must be a dream." Once prompted to lucid awareness, you can begin to explore the dream consciously.

Together, these three gateways constitue a vast array of techniques and approaches for increasing the frequency of your lucid dreams. Here are a few more helpful methods to achieving lucid dreams.

MILD (*Mnemonic Induction of Lucid Dreams*)
The early pioneer of lucid dream research, Stephen LaBerge, felt that the "intention to remember" to become lucid seemed of particular

importance when inducing lucid dreams. LaBerge developed a memory technique that he called the Mnemonic Induction of Lucid Dreams (MILD).[43] The MILD technique has four basic steps:

Memorize your last dream in detail when you spontaneously wake up at night.

Insert yourself becoming lucid at an appropriate point in the remembered dream.

Lucidly intend to become aware in your next dream by suggesting: "Next time I'm dreaming, I want to recognize I'm dreaming."

Determine to repeat the preceding steps until you feel prepared to succeed. Expect to become lucid and aware in your next dream as you fall back asleep.

I had been lucid dreaming for more than six years when I first heard of this technique. When I began to use it, my lucid dreams doubled in frequency. Although LaBerge focuses on memory as the primary factor, some feel MILD's role-playing and revisualization may have equal importance, as you will see in this next practice.

How to Practice for MILD

On a sheet of paper, write down a recent dream.

• Identify with a large X an appropriate place in your dream story that could have prompted lucid awareness (a strange event, an impossible action, an odd situation, or an unlikely place).

• Using the large X as your starting point, rewrite the dream as if you had become lucid.

For example, if you dreamed you were in Central Park and saw an elephant with wings, put an X at that unusual spot in your dream and proceed to rewrite:

> Seeing an elephant with wings (X), I thought: "Wait a second; elephants do not have wings! This must be a dream." Now lucid, I remembered that I wished to fly. I looked around and saw the Empire State Building. I focused on the top of it and began flying like Superman to the very top. It was cool to look down and see how far I had flown.

Again, you need to remember to perform these four actions for MILD when you spontaneously awaken at night: Memorize your last dream; insert yourself becoming lucid at an appropriate point; lucidly suggest, "The next time I am dreaming, I want to recognize I am dreaming"; and determine to do it as you fall back asleep.

Paul Tholey's Critical Reflection Technique

In 1959, German Gestalt psychologist Paul Tholey developed a method for becoming lucidly aware in a dream. For weeks, he asked himself about ten times a day: "Am I dreaming or not?" Then he asked: "How do I know?" He really thought about these questions, believing that this questioning attitude would transfer to his dreaming mind. It took about a month of repeating the questions before he saw a deceased relative in a dream and wondered: "Am I dreaming?"

People have called this the Critical Question or the Critical Reflection Technique, since it relies on daytime reflective questioning to carry over and continue in the dream state.[44] Some have suggested putting a red C (for "conscious") on their hands with a marker and, each time they see it during the day, asking themselves: "Am I dreaming or not?" Others have created reality-checking applications that beep at random times, prompting them to question their state of awareness. They can then do a reality check like trying to levitate. Eventually, they hope that this persistent questioning will transfer to their dream state.

In my opinion, Paul Tholey has touched on one piece of a larger idea, which I call *developing a lucid mindset*. This idea came to me as I wondered why a few select people have ultra-frequent lucid dreams (literally 1,000 lucid dreams a year). I noticed that many ultra-frequent lucid dreamers stated that they had recurring childhood nightmares and learned how to become lucid as a means to escape them. After that, they could discern the dream state easily and become lucid nightly.

Developing a lucid mindset means establishing a persistent mental habit of reexamining your perceived environment or state of awareness. Whether ultra-frequent lucid dreamers rely on memory (e.g., What was I just doing?), vigilance (e.g., Am I safe here from the monsters?), location (e.g., Where am I?), or critical questioning (e.g., Am I dreaming at this moment?), they have a mental habit of repeatedly checking or analyzing their current situation or state of mind and, as a result, becoming lucidly aware. In short, they rely on a lucid mindset as a powerful technique for inducing lucid dreams.

You can actually develop a lucid mindset by using any daytime questioning that elevates your awareness. I developed the habit of seeing the world as a kind of mental co-creation of the conscious and unconscious mind. When something happens, I ask myself: "Why did this happen to me? What beliefs do I have that attracted this event into my life?" Later, when something strange happens in a dream, I think: "Why did that happen? How did I attract it into my life?" Then I realize: "This seems too strange. This must be a dream!"

How to Develop a Lucid Mindset

Developing a lucid mindset is easy and can help you achieve awareness in your dreams, yet it requires persistence and the proper inquiring attitude.

- Establish a mental habit of critical questioning that appeals to you and causes you to reexamine your perceived environment or your state of awareness. Create your own critical question (e.g. Where am I? How did I get here?).

- Actively engage in this mental investigation many times throughout the day so that it becomes second nature—a true habit.

- After a bit of time, your new mental habit will emerge in your thinking even when you dream, which will cause you to examine things more closely and come to the realization: "This is a dream!"

WILD (*Wake Initiated Lucid Dreams*)

Beverly Kedzierski Heart D'Urso served as LaBerge's main lucid dreaming research subject, or oneironaut, for many years. Because film crews often had to stay up all night to film her while lucid dreaming, she decided to make it easier on everyone by asking them to come early in the morning, when REM seems more prevalent. After waking naturally in the morning, Beverly taught herself to move directly from the waking state to the lucid dreaming state. She simply closed her eyes and consciously waited for a dream scene to arise. Seeing the dream imagery, she would then move her awareness into it. Various film crews caught this event on tape as she fell asleep and then signaled her conscious awareness with her eyes while lucid dreaming.

Beverly recalls that LaBerge gave this action the name WILD—for Wake Initiated Lucid Dreaming—because of its similarity to his own technique of MILD, or Mnemonic Induction of Lucid Dreams.[45] The WILD technique has come to refer to any method that helps you take your waking awareness directly into the sleep state to become lucidly aware in a dream. Various approaches can help you accomplish this, like the counting technique suggested by LaBerge and given here.

Count Down to Lucidity

- Select a time when you feel naturally drowsy, like a normal nap-time during the day or after waking in the middle of the night.

- As you close your eyes and begin to drift off to sleep, count mentally: "One, I am dreaming. Two, I am dreaming. Three, I am dreaming," and so on.

- Eventually, you may find yourself in a dream-like setting, mentally saying: "Twenty-one, I am dreaming." And you realize that you are.

Another approach involves adopting the attitude of a detached observer.

- With a quiet mind and closed eyes, let yourself begin to drift off as you passively observe colors move about and shift.

- Remain observant, waiting for dream images to form.

- When a dream collects, mentally enter the imagery's environment and actively establish your lucid awareness.

Ed Kellogg has found success with a similar technique in which he concentrates on his breathing as he falls asleep. By maintaining a focused awareness on his inhalations and exhalations as he moves into sleep, he can often carry his awareness across and realize that dream imagery has formed. Then, through a mental effort, he moves his awareness into the dream and becomes established there lucidly.

I have noticed that, sometimes, this movement of awareness into a dream feels literally like pulling your awareness into a new space. For example, it sometimes feels like pulling yourself into a room from a nearby space or climbing out of a hole into a broader space. For some, it may appear as moving through a tunnel. Prepare yourself to make that movement from the role of passive observer to a new role as a lucid, active participant in the dream space.

CRAM (*Constant Repetition and Affirmation Method*)

Most college students are familiar with cramming for a test—stuffing their short-term memories with important bits of information. Similarly, I have observed that falling asleep while constantly affirming the intention to become lucidly aware may place that intent in your short-term memory and promote lucid dreaming. I came to call my idea the Constant Repetition and Affirmation Method, or CRAM.

CRAM Your Way to Lucidity

- As you fall asleep, or awaken at night and fall back to sleep, softly express your intention in your mind: "Tonight, I will become lucidly aware" (or some similar simple suggestion).

- Repeat this intent over and over. Let it flood your mind and become your primary intent as you return to sleep.

- Do this in a relaxed and peaceful manner that allows you to enter the sleep state with this active intention in mind.

- If your mind drifts, gently bring it back to this constant, gentle repetition.

WBTB (*Wake Back to Bed Technique*)

This method of induction has been independently noticed by many lucid dreamers and confirmed as extremely powerful by a research study at the Lucidity Institute. Also called the Nap to Lucidity Technique, it significantly increases the probability of a lucid dream.

For people using this technique, the number of lucid dreams skyrocketed in the final sleep period, compared to baseline records. In fact, the Lucidity Institute study showed that you are five to ten times more likely to become lucid when using this technique.[46]

During the waking period, some people prefer to meditate, whereas others read about lucid dreaming and then fall back asleep with the intent to lucid dream. In addition, lucid dreamers report success with this after spending from fifteen to forty five minutes awake. Find an amount of time that works for you. Even those who struggle with a bit of insomnia note that they have a tendency to become lucid after tossing and turning for a while.

The WBTB technique's success has resulted in various adaptations, notably the Cycle Adjustment Technique (CAT), proposed by Daniel Love in his book *Are You Dreaming?*[47] Also, some lucid dreamers have found success with polyphasic sleeping, or changing the wake/sleep pattern to allow for multiple sleep times throughout the day.

Nap Your Way to Lucidity

- Wake about two hours before your normal waking time.

- Spend the next fifteen to forty-five minutes awake, possibly reading or thinking about lucid dreaming, or meditating.

- Return to sleep with the intent to become lucid.

Dream Re-entry

Have you ever wakened from a marvelous dream wishing you could re-enter it? Actually, you can. Working independently around the globe, dreamers and lucid dreamers have identified the characteristic actions that enable you to re-enter a dream from which you have just awakened. Often, a lucid dream will restart at this point and carry you along lucidly, just as if you had skipped ten seconds in a videotape.

How to Re-enter a Dream

After waking from a dream or lucid dream, use these steps to re-enter it:

- Get your physical body in the exact position you were in upon waking. Or, better yet, do not move at all upon waking.

- With your eyes closed, imagine the end of the dream (or the last fifteen seconds), as if looking at a picture or movie.

- Let this image become real-seeming to you (you may re-enter at this point and the lucid dream may begin). Or choose an item or dream figure to cast your awareness into and begin perceiving the dream from this vantage point. Allow the dream to continue.

Keep Practicing

All these techniques will have little value if you do not practice them, so step into the game in a way that appeals to you. Have fun with it. Don't worry about instant success. See how close you get. Create a positive and supportive belief in your ability to lucid dream.

In workshops, I watch people making the effort and taking the beginning steps to achieve this. Some have never had a lucid dream before in their lives. Some have reached retirement age and want to learn some new tricks. Incredibly, many of them succeed, and celebrate joyfully when they do become lucid. Behind their success lies practice.

It helps to examine your dreams more closely as you seek a fully lucid dream. Did you have a dream with a moment of critical awareness? Did you think something seemed odd? Or did a helpful dream figure appear and begin to act in a way that made you question your surroundings? Those dreams sound very close to sub-lucid or semi-lucid dreams and show that your intent to elevate your critical awareness has reached your subconscious.

Pay attention to the small steps and details, because, one night, you may see something like a dinosaur walking through the book stacks of your library or your hands popping up in front of your face, and you will realize that it all leads to one undeniable conclusion: "This must be a dream!"

Chapter 4

STABILIZING YOUR LUCID DREAMS

So you have joyfully announced: "Hey, this is a dream!" What happens next? For many beginning lucid dreamers, their success depends on how they respond in those first thirty seconds. In those early crucial moments, there are important steps you can take to set you on the path to an exciting and lengthy lucid dream. Properly and firmly establishing your conscious awareness in the initial moments of lucidity is the primary goal of my MEME method.

MEME

Shifting from regular dreaming to the sudden realization of lucid dreaming can seem quite a dramatic switch, especially at the beginning. Fortunately, there are simple guidelines that can help you make a smooth and successful transiton. These four simple techniques of the MEME method will allow you to stabilize both your mind and your lucid dream:

Modulate your emotions

Enhance your awareness

Maintain your focus

Establish your intent or goal

Following these four easy steps will help you extend the duration of your lucid dreaming and allow you to maximize your lucid dreaming experience. I encourage all beginners to memorize these steps in order to be prepared when they realize, "This is a lucid dream!"

Modulate Your Emotions

If you feel too excited on becoming lucid, be prepared to do one of the following to calm yourself:

- Mentally tell yourself to "calm down" to reduce the feeling of excitation.

- Visually focus on something boring like your hands, your feet, the floor, or any emotionally neutral visual scene.

- Concentrate your energies on a simple task to reduce the level of sensed emotion.

Because many people find that excess emotions have a tendency to end the lucid dreaming experience, try to avoid becoming too excited. If you do feel overly emotional, use the preceding ideas to decrease the emotional charge and remain lucid. By using these ideas to modulate your emotions, you will bypass the primary beginner's mistake and have a longer lucid dream.

Sometimes, however, you may wish to do something really exciting or emotionally powerful. In those instances, try waiting and performing that activity at the very end of a long lucid dream, since the intense emotion may cause you to wake.

Enhance Your Awareness

For beginners, increasing your awareness at the onset of lucidity seems to be a good basic practice. Consider doing the following to increase your awareness:

- Perform a reality check—levitate, put your hand through a wall, or pull your finger and make it longer—to prove you are dreaming.

- Engage in a solidifying ritual like rubbing your hands together to activate your kinesthetic senses.

- Shout out a suggestion to the dream: "Greater clarity now!" or "More lucid awareness!"

Most of us notice occasional lucid dreams in which the lighting seems very dim at the beginning. When I shout "Greater clarity now" or "More lucid awareness," the lighting in the lucid dream suddenly improves a great deal, as if someone has heard my request and adjusted the brightness of the lights. Try it yourself if you ever become lucid in a low-light situation.

Similarly, rubbing your hands together can make you feel more present and aware in a lucid dream. That actions seems to affirm that you exist consciously within the dream. An elevated awareness makes the next goal of maintaining your focus much easier.

Maintain Your Focus

Of all the issues that perplex new lucid dreamers, maintaining focus seems the primary challenge. Some become lucid and feel very amazed by knowing they exist within a dream. Then, as they go to explore in the dream, they find very interesting objects or situations or dream figures. As they attend to these dream elements, they can lose their awareness and their knowledge of lucidity, and slide into unaware dreaming. In waking life and in lucid dreaming, awareness fluctuates. Just because you *become* lucid does not mean that you will *remain* lucid.

You must engage the lucid dream action as it happens, while simultaneously maintaining your awareness of being lucid. You have to remain both *in the dream* and *in your awareness of the dreaming*. Thus, you need to perform at two levels simultaneously. On one level, you maintain your meta-cognitive awareness of dreaming; on the other level, you interact with the dream events and figures. Like an actor on the stage, you must engage the other actors, while realizing that it is a play in which you perform.

Some lucid dreamers perform repetitive actions to remind themselves that they are dreaming. For instance, every fifteen seconds, they may announce: "This is a lucid dream." Or they may perform other repetitive actions at certain intervals (e.g., levitate). A friend told me that she sometimes begins singing a song in her lucid dreams, which focuses her energies and maintains her lucidity. For most people, it also helps to stay active, because the process of making decisions keeps your powers of conscious deliberation and lucid awareness active.

One caution about focus: Avoid staring at objects in a lucid dream. For some reason, many lucid dreamers find that staring fixedly at something for more than four or five seconds can cause the dream to feel shaky and then visually to collapse. If you want to examine something, look at it briefly and then turn away for a few seconds before coming back to it. For example, look at a painting, then look at your hands, and then look back at the painting.

Establish Your Intent or Goal

Particularly for beginners, I urge you to maintain your focus by establishing a simple intent or goal to accomplish in the lucid dream. After you accomplish your first goal, establish a new intent or goal immediately and try to accomplish it next. A series of simple goals—for instance, touch the wall, then touch your arm, then pinch your arm, then talk to a dream figure, then ask what it represents, then listen for a response—works well for beginners. Select goals that interest you.

By constantly re-focusing on new goals, you maintain an active state of awareness and an active engagement of the dream. Without an active focus on a goal, two things may happen. You may lose your awareness of lucidity and become entranced by the dream. Or new dream figures, objects, or activities may spontaneously enter the dream (probably created from your unconscious layer of awareness). You may find these newly inserted items interesting, lose lucidity, and begin regular dreaming.

More advanced lucid dreamers simply recall a goal or experiment conceived in waking hours—seeking a creative solution to a problem at work, directing healing energy onto a physical ailment, or seeing what it is like to meditate within a lucid dream. Once recalled, they can then try to actualize that goal. Others use the goal of exploring and literally spend their entire lucid dream examining everything they come across. When you have active goals, you will find it easier to stay lucid longer.

Experimenting in Lucid Dreams

If you wish to conduct an experiment in a lucid dream, plan it in the waking state. Why? Sometimes, people report having a difficult time deciding how to perform an experiment in a lucid dream. Or, in the joy of the lucid dream itself, they report creating an experiment that does not provide convincing evidence to the waking self. By planning an experiment ahead of time, you know exactly what you intend to do and how you can do it.

For example, Ed Kellogg, who has deeply investigated the potential for physical healing in lucid dreams, sought some way to recall, practically and accurately, his waking intent to perform a particular healing experiment in his next lucid dream.[48] So, in the waking state, he created a rhyming chant based on his intended goal and memorized it, such as this:

Now let the healing energy shine,
To cure the lungs with power divine.

When he became lucid, Kellogg recalled his task and the chant easily because of his waking preparation. He realized that doing this in the waking state helped him remember the waking experiment or intent once lucid. This allowed him to focus his intent more powerfully. By creating the approach while awake, lucid dreamers don't wonder what to do or how to do it when lucid. They know and act directly to realize their goals. A simple practice like *pre*-creating your planned intent and action may help you recall and achieve your lucid dreaming goals.

How to Create Successful Plans

List three goals that you want to perform in a lucid dream. Now select one of the three goals and describe how you will achieve it. Be specific.

If creating a phrase to focus your intent, what phrase will encapsulate your intent? Write it down. By mentally practicing in the waking state, you help *pre*-create the conditions for a successful outcome.

═══

Prolonging Lucid Dreams

Lucid dreamers have employed various methods to prolong dreams that seem ready to collapse or end. The indicators of a lucid dream's imminent collapse include the dream seeming shaky or visually blurry, or the dreamer realizing that he or she feels too much emotion. On some level, lucid dreamers often know intuitively that their dreams are ready to collapse unless action is taken.

The following methods describe techniques that many have used to keep their lucid dreams going, even when their dreams seem ready to collapse.

Find your hands: In Carlos Castaneda's book *Journey to Ixtlan*, his shamanic teacher, don Juan, told him to look back at his hands to renew the power of dreaming if the dream seemed ready to collapse.[49] I have done this successfully on a number of occasions. I shift my focus back to my hands for a few seconds and find it very calming and centering. Somehow, the lucid dream seems restabilized, and I can continue with my exploring or experimenting.

Spin or fall backward: Stephen LaBerge found that you could often prolong a lucid dream by spinning or falling backward. This activity may prolong your awareness or possibly create a new lucid dream setting. In fact, he found that spinning resulted in a new dream setting about 85 percent of the time.[50] Because actions in lucid dreams have some corresponding physical effects, LaBerge wondered whether spinning activated the vestibular system (associated with balance), which may positively affect the dreaming process and prolong the lucid dream. When he taught this practice to others, he noticed that the power of their expectation often brought them to a new dream setting.

Grab on to something: If your dreamscape or visual imagery starts to fade away into a sparkling black emptiness, grab onto something in the dream—your dream body or a dream object. Hold on tight and focus your attention on what it feels like, even if the visual aspect of the dream completely disappears and you find yourself in a sparkling black void. After a while, if you maintain your awareness, the dreamscape will very likely reappear around you. Bit by bit, the visual images of a new lucid dream will emerge.

Touch something: Various lucid dreamers have found that the kinesthetic sense of touching something keeps your focus active while in this void state. Many have also found that simply keeping your mind active can maintain your presence in this state until a new lucid dream forms around you. It may take a minute or more, but if you hang in there, you can watch the birth of a dream scene.

Close your eyes: Some lucid dreamers have reported success at keeping their lucid dreams going by closing their dream eyes briefly or falling down. These actions apparently help some prolong the dream state or create a new dream scene when a dream seems ready to collapse.

Waking from Lucid Dreams

When dreamers wish to wake from lucid dreams, most simply decide or intend to wake up, and they do so easily. They just tell themselves to wake up, and they do. It's literally that simple.

Others know they will wake if they stare at one object in a dream for five seconds. Still others know that, if they engage in certain emotion-producing behaviors while lucid, they will likely wake.

In general, lucid dreamers have no problem waking. Most are more concerned about staying in their dreams and avoiding things that make them end. Of course, when a lucid dream ends, three things can happen:

• You most likely wake in bed.

• You have a false awakening.

• You find yourself in an imageless state—the black sparkling state often called "the void"—and then wake up in bed.

A false awakening is the experience of believing that you have woken from a lucid dream only to realize that you continue to dream.[51] For example, you have a wonderful lucid dream, get too excited, expect to wake up, and then find yourself in bed where you see your lucid dream written in the dream journal. Who wrote the dream down? Then it hits you; you are still dreaming! With that realization, you normally awaken to physical reality immediately.

Some people use the realization of a false awakening to conduct a reality check and begin a new lucid dream. Experienced lucid dreamers also realize that, although a lucid dream seems finished and they find themselves in bed, it just may be a false awakening. So each time you believe you have awakened from a lucid dream, try a reality check like levitating or pulling your finger to see if it elongates. You may find that your finger does elongate, and then you can use the false-awakening state to continue your lucid adventure.

The third ending to a lucid dream involves the dream collapsing and you finding yourself aware in a visually empty space of sparkling blackness or void. Many find this space very relaxing. It may remind some of the sparkling blackness on an old-fashioned television set, when the channels signed off for the night. If you maintain your lucid awareness in this void state, you can often watch a new lucid dream pop up around you.

Most beginners (but not all) will probably tell you that their lucid dreams last less than five minutes. Some intermediate lucid dreamers find that they can remain lucid for up to fifteen minutes. Experienced lucid dreamers can go beyond that time; some sleep labs report observing as much as fifty minutes or more of continuous lucid dreaming, based on eye signaling by an experienced dreamer.

Please note that experienced lucid dreamers often voluntarily cut short the length of their dreams because of the difficulty in remembering all the events of a long-lasting lucid dream. When they conduct a lucid dreaming experiment, they normally tell themselves to awaken after getting the experimental results so they can easily recall them. One cognitive challenge of lucid dreaming involves remembering details clearly; thus, when you receive the results of your personal experiment, tell yourself to wake up while they remain clear in your mind.

The Physical Senses in Lucid Dreaming

The sensory experience of lucid dreaming has many interesting facets. While awake, you rely on your physical senses. You pull an apple off a tree, feel its weight, and see its apple-colored surface. You press the skin and smell the apple scent. Opening it, you bite and chew a section, tasting its juicy sweetness and, if you drop it, you hear it fall to the ground with a *thud*. For you, these sensory experiences confirm the reality of the apple.

Part of the beauty of lucid dreaming involves the sensory reality of the lucid dream experience. For the most part, this seems as real as when you are awake. Your arm feels real. Your favorite cotton T-shirt feels like your favorite cotton T-shirt. Your friend, John, looks just like he does in the waking state, right down to the slight gap between his two front teeth. Because of this similarity to waking reality, you must stay vigilant and aware that you exist within a dream (and, of course, you can do a reality check if you need to convince yourself or re-convince yourself). Altogether, however, you see your sensory faculties in a new role, as helpful fabricators of your lucid dream experience in keeping with your beliefs, expectations, and feelings. They normally follow your unstated direction.

When you are consciously aware in a lucid dream, however, you can mindfully experiment with sensory experience and see exactly how your lucid dream senses compare to your waking senses. Will a lucid dream apple smell the same and taste the same as the waking version? How will a well-known piece of music sound in a lucid dream, and how will it touch you emotionally there? What about a lucid dream kiss? Better? Worse? Or just different?

As a lucid dream explorer, consider testing your five basic physical senses while lucid dreaming and comparing them to waking physical reality. For each sense, make a detailed comparison:

Sight: How similar? How different? Do colors seem deeper and richer in waking reality or in lucid dreaming?

Touch: How similar? How different? Do the surfaces of things seem the same? What about the weight?

Taste: How similar? How different? Does it matter whether the item is sweet, sour, bitter, or salty?

Smell: How similar? How different? Does it matter whether the smell seems pleasing or disgusting?

Hearing: How similar? How different? Does the hearing occur in your mind or through your ears? Or both?

Did any of your senses become accentuated in the lucid dream state beyond the normal range? Did any of your senses become diminished in the lucid dream state? Did your sensory experience change as you changed your thinking or beliefs about it?

If you like to do comparison and contrast studies, investigate other sensations in your lucid dreams—temperature, pain, balance, or motion. How do they compare in a lucid dream? Moreover, can you use lucid dreaming to become the sensed item? What does it feel like to become an apple?

Extra Credit for Extrasensory Experience

Now that you have compared and contrasted your physical senses between the waking and lucid dreaming states, try to alter your sensed experience in a lucid dream through the power of belief and expectation. For example, in a lucid dream, bite into an orange while telling yourself: "I expect this to taste like a banana!" Or, in a lucid dream, pinch yourself very hard while telling yourself: "I expect my dream body to be oblivious to pain!"

When you seek to alter your sensory experience through expectation, what happens to the experience? What happens to the orange's taste when you actively expect it to taste like a banana? Does a hard pinch feel like nothing when you consciously intend it to? More broadly, to what degree does expectation influence your lucid dreaming experience? What does this suggest about the nature of the senses as infallible reporters of truth?

In waking, you may feel that your physical senses are hard-wired. But in lucid dreaming, you see that sensory experience is easily modified by mental activity. This suggests that your physical senses may be trained to function as they do.

In the second half of this book, we will go further than most lucid dreaming books and explore the interior of lucid dreams—the experience of lucid dreaming in the moment. By examining visible dream objects, dream settings, and dream figures along with the mental activity of your conscious and unconscious mind, you will develop a more advanced understanding of what helps create lucid dreams. With those insights, you can realize how to access the amazing potential of lucid dreaming for personal growth, health, and transformation.

Chapter 5

THE POWER OF PROJECTION

Mark, a sports science student in Germany, knew he had only modest skills as a swimmer.[52] Even that statement was perhaps too generous. According to sources, Mark's swimming coach had told him: "Mark, you are a stone. You will never be a good swimmer." Yet Mark had one skill the swimming coach did not realize—he had frequent lucid dreams.

To earn a better grade in the bi-weekly class, Mark began to practice swimming in his lucid dreams. To prepare, he watched videos of good swimming form on the Internet and then, at night, recalled that information in his lucid dreams, when he copied the improved techniques and better style. Nightly, he began his swimming practice whenever lucid. For example, Mark focused solely on the proper way to plunge his right arm into the water and felt relieved that he could concentrate on this in a lucid dream without gasping for air or swallowing water.

During class, Mark asked his swim coach for some additional pointers on swimming technique. The coach watched him swim and was surprised by his rapid improvement. From one class session to the next, he just seemed to get better. This lucid dreaming stone began to show potential as a swimmer.

Mark likely did not tell his coach everything he did in those lucid dreams. Once, while lucid dreaming, Mark transformed the pool's water into substances like yogurt or honey so he could swim through these thick liquids, feel the resistance, and build up endurance. In other instances, he lucidly swam through air and bubbles to get his swimming stroke correct and see how it moved him through space.

Using dreaming's creative potential, he even reports lucidly swimming through a pool of Gummi Bears.

Melanie Schädlich, lucid dream researcher at the University of Heidelberg, interviewed Mark about improving his athletic performance through lucid dreaming. Schädlich reports that Mark sometimes used his skills to change his perspective within a lucid dream. For example, he lucidly watched his dream self swim from a perspective above him to see how his technique looked from that angle. Or he cast his awareness to the side to see whether his swimming form needed improvement. Mark used these new perspectives in his lucid dreams to learn and synchronize the complex body movements of swimming.[53]

Through lucid dreaming, Mark worked on realizing his waking intent. He moved from swimming "like a stone" to getting high marks in both swim skills and time. Moreover, he taught others by example (like his swimming coach) that lucid dreaming has extraordinary potential when thoughtfully applied and mastered.

How you learn to move in lucid dreams often illustrates the depth of your understanding about this special state. In Mark's case, he had a clear goal to achieve and used his lucid dreaming skills to manipulate space and practice skill-building. He knew that, in a lucid dream, a swimming pool can contain anything you consciously project into it: yogurt, honey, air, bubbles, and even Gummi Bears. The conscious use of mental projection can actively change your experienced environment.

Moreover, Mark used his lucid dreaming skills to do another kind of projecting. He projected his awareness into his coach to get a different perspective on his swimming technique, and he projected his awareness above and to the side to observe his swimming form. These kinds of projections show the abilities of lucid dreamers to manipulate both space and their awareness within it by the active power of projecting.

Your Projected Mental Overlay

To succeed as a lucid dreamer requires understanding projection. In fact, you will probably need to deal with your own passive projections first—that mixture of unexamined beliefs, feelings, and untested assumptions that you unthinkingly project outward onto your lucid dreams. I call this rarely noticed mental activity a lucid dreamer's "projected mental overlay."

In the waking world, you sometimes see extreme examples of people who project their inner issues onto their experience. A paranoid person feels utterly convinced that the mail carrier secretly spies on him (along with all other government officials). A hypochondriac sees potential health threats in common body sensations or a neighbor's simple cough. An introvert feels isolated and ignored in a lonely world, even when invited to join in the conversation at a family reunion.

You can see how these mental beliefs are often projected outward and overlaid onto everyday events. For example, a paranoid person sees the mail carrier talking and laughing with a neighbor, Mrs. Smith, and becomes convinced that she acts as a government informant. Without realizing it, these simple events are interpreted to conform to and confirm our belief systems, which in turn color our perception.

Although extreme examples of this get our attention, we may fail to notice how we all routinely project our mental overlay of ideas, beliefs, feelings, and expectations onto other individuals, cultures, and situations. They may seem like small assumptions and prejudices, but they influence our perspective, interpretation, and response to life. In many respects, we do not interact with the world as *it* exists; rather we interact with the world as *we* exist, psychologically and philosophically.

Your belief system also plays a critical function in the inner space of lucid dreaming. Your projected mental overlay of ideas, beliefs, feelings, and expectations is invisibly layered over lucid dream figures, objects, settings, and events. You may not even notice this, so to succeed at lucid dreaming requires that you see how your projected mental overlay works and what it tells you about the underlying principles of lucid dreaming.

Let's look at some examples that involve moving in the lucid dream space. Reread this lucid dream from chapter 2 and watch what happens when the woman changes her projected mental overlay.

I saw a clock moving backward and thought: "This is a dream!" Then I remembered that I heard on the radio a lucid dreaming expert say: "In a lucid dream, gravity does not exist." Suddenly, I floated up to the ceiling and could not get down!

Do you see what happens? As soon as she recalls the idea that, in a lucid dream, gravity does not exist, she begins to float. Two vitally important lessons in lucidity emerge here:

- The dream space largely mirrors your ideas, expectations, feelings, and beliefs about it.

- When you change your ideas, expectations, and beliefs (or your projected mental overlay), your experience normally changes.

As soon as this lucid dreamer internally realizes that gravity has no meaning in a lucid dream, she floats to the ceiling. She does not have to flap her arms or intend herself to the ceiling; she only changes her belief about the situation, and then her experience mirrors her new thinking.

However, what about the moment before that realization, when her lucid dream feet seem firmly planted on the floor? Here, you see the constant, invisibly active nature of projected mental overlay. She experiences the lucid dream in accordance with whatever conscious or subconscious beliefs operate *at that moment.* In effect, her belief system invisibly overlays the dream space. But when she examines her thinking and recalls that gravity does not exist in a lucid dream, she immediately experiences the newly realized belief and floats to the ceiling effortlessly.

In lucid dreams, your projected mental overlay invisibly radiates outward from you, which then affects both you (the perceiver) and almost all of your perceived experience. You can confirm this by changing your ideas, beliefs, and expectations in a lucid dream and seeing how the dream objects and setting respond. If changing your mind results in changing the dream, you can safely conclude that a linkage exists. Understanding this linkage can illuminate both your dreaming and your waking awareness.

While lucid dreaming, you often notice the subtle nature of your thoughts. For example, you see a dream figure in a big leather overcoat, which reminds you of something that a gangster might wear. With that association, you now wonder whether this dream figure seems dangerous. The dream figure turns around, and it looks as if he has a knife. Lucid, you decide to fly away.

You can change your thinking and expectations in this lucid dream, however, and decide that lots of very nice people wear big leather overcoats. With that newly projected mental overlay, you will likely encounter someone nice and friendly in that coat. Your dream experience reflects you in that moment and is created by the subtle nature of these mental responses.

In many regards, you have an invisible projector inside of you that beams out the mental energy of your beliefs, feelings, and expectations in response to whatever dream situation you experience. That mental energy often coalesces into dream objects and settings for you to experience in each moment. Like Mark, the lucid dreaming swimmer, you can use the power of projection to accomplish your actively intended goals. Understanding these passive projections first will help you clear the path to becoming an accomplished lucid dreamer.

Moving in Dream Space

The amazing freedom and joy of flying in lucid dreams brings inexpressible happiness to many lucid dreamers. To fly freely around a dream like a bird or a superhero feels awesome, visually incredible, and completely thrilling. But for some beginners, flying can seem frustrating as well.

I recall my first attempt at flying. Becoming lucid in the front yard by a sycamore tree, I decided to fly. Not knowing how, I leap into the air and hang there about four feet off the ground. A bit bewildered, I then decided to swim through the air doing the breaststroke to make some progress. I did this for about a minute and stopped to see how far I had traveled. Looking down at the ground fifteen feet below me, I became fearful about falling from this height. Suddenly, I fell and hit the soft, almost rubbery, ground. Drat.

In those early days, I tried other methods of flying in lucid dreaming space. Sometimes I flapped my arms like a bird and managed to fly around a bit. Sometimes I began running to gain momentum, put my arms out like airplane wings, and flew around until I lost the momentum and hit the ground. All these attempts seemed short-lived and unfulfilling.

After a couple of years of this, a moment of sudden insight arrived: Swimming through the air, flapping your arms, or running to glide all require physical effort. But physical effort only makes sense in a physical environment. Therefore, I needed to let go of ideas of physical effort when aware in a lucid dream.

To move intelligently and quickly in the mental space of lucid dreams, you need to switch to mental approaches to movement. Lucid dreaming occurs in a mentally responsive space. By manipulating your mind, you can move through mental space more easily. Letting go of the idea of physical effort and the limiting beliefs of physical motion will lead to liberation from self-adopted constraints about dream space.

How to Move in Dream Space

- Intend to levitate yourself.

- Remind yourself that, in a lucid dream, physical gravity does not exist.

- See what happens when you stop and think: "I'm in a lucid dream; therefore, gravity does not exist."

- Do you levitate?

- Do you feel liberated from gravity or from the idea of gravity? What happens to you at that moment?

In a lucid dream, you can tie yourself to physically oriented experience when you hold a belief in it or subconsciously expect it. However, in the reality of dream space, you can experiment with a new type of physics based on mental principles. As you will learn in mental physics, the apple falls in a lucid dream by virtue of the perceiver's consciousness (i.e., mental beliefs and expectations), because physical gravity does not exist in the dream state. If you do not wish the apple to fall—or, better yet, *if you do not wish to fall yourself*—change your mind (i.e., your beliefs and expectations). See what happens.

The Role of Emotions

Although physical gravity does not exist in lucid dreams, a kind of mental and emotional gravity does (e.g., focus on fear, doubt in abilities). Like many beginning lucid dreamers, I noticed an occasional early lucid dream in which I flew with grace and ease. I soared through the air, dove toward the ground, banked left and right, did loops and rolls that Harry Potter would envy. At other times, I was less successful. Why did lucid flying sometimes seem so easy and at other times so laborious?

Reflecting on these experiences, I realized that, when I expected to have difficulty flying, I did. When I feared I might fall to the ground, I normally fell. Therefore, my feelings and expectations projected out from me, overlaid the dream, and became a large factor in my lucid dream experience.

Conversely, when I felt buoyantly exuberant, I flew like a master of the skies. When I expected to have an amazing flight, I normally had an amazing flight. When I knew without a doubt that gravity did not exist in the dream state, I could float upside down, lie sideways, and even walk on the air. Mastering flight in a lucid dream involves a kind of mental self-mastery, and joyful emotions indicate the inner congruence between intent and beliefs.

These insights touch on another aspect of emotions within lucid dreams: feeling conflicted. Let's say you become lucidly aware and feel a sudden urge to smoke in a lucid dream, even though you have given up smoking in waking life. Now, in the dream, you feel a bit conflicted as you go off to get some dream cigarettes. Suddenly, you notice that you can barely move! It feels as if you are walking in wet concrete. What happened?

Inner conflicts sometimes express themselves as difficulty in moving in lucid dreams. A founder of social psychology, Kurt Lewin, calls this type of inner dilemma an *approach/avoidance conflict,* because you simultaneously want to do and do not want to do the action. In lucid dreams, sluggish movement reflects an inner emotional conflict of wanting to do something, but worrying about expressing the experience. As you get closer to it, you may find that movement becomes even more difficult as the negative energy or consequence increases in your mind.

Again, these two important lessons can help structure your lucid experience:

- The dream space largely mirrors your ideas, expectations, feelings, and beliefs about it.

- When you change your ideas, expectations, feelings, and beliefs—your projected mental overlay—your experience normally changes.

It may take you a while to see that moving successfully in the mental space of lucid dreaming has various components, like your beliefs, expectations, and emotions. Although your feelings normally follow in line with your beliefs, you can possess conflicting beliefs of varying magnitudes. When you have conflicting beliefs, the clear expression of mental energy becomes fractured and impedes your traditional movement or progress.

The Power of Projected Belief

In fact, lucid dreamers can use the power of projected belief to move within the lucid dream space. How? By investing a dream object with the power of flight or movement and strongly believing this. They can then use this newly empowered object to take them flying around the dream.

For example, in a lucid dream long ago, I noticed a big blue sandal (twice as big as normal). For some reason, I decided that this big blue sandal could fly and take me wherever I wanted to go. I truly believed this. I touched the sandal and, suddenly, it began flying as I held on! It took me to the places that I wished. I felt amazement, because this blue sandal moved very quickly.

Upon waking, I realized that, even though the sandal did have some symbolic connection with moving and walking, my belief in its power to fly was the necessary factor or the active ingredient that empowered it to fly. Without that empowering belief, a blue sandal seems just a blue sandal. However, when you empower it by sincere belief while lucid, it becomes a rocket.

In another case, I became lucid and noticed an airplane nearby. Understanding the power of projecting belief into a dream object, I decided that, if I touched the airplane, it could fly me around the dream scene. I touched the airplane, which levitated and began flying me wherever I focused on going. As long as I held on (and believed), it effortlessly took me to various places.

The power of projected belief emerges in the earlier lucid dream of the woman who rented a pair of cheap wings to go flying. As she held the wings and flew around, she ultimately realized that, whenever she doubted the cheap wings, she plummeted to the ground. But when she believed in their power to fly, she could fly easily around the lucid dreamscape.

Her story helps illustrate how our projected mental overlays dramatically (or dream-atically) affect our experience. You can believe a little or a lot. You can doubt a little or a lot. And although you often subconsciously project your mental overlay, you can consciously project it as well. Whatever conscious or unconscious mental stance you take normally ends up projected and reflected back into your experience.

As Buckaroo Banzai, in the movie *The Adventures of Buckaroo Banzai*, succinctly stated: "No matter where you go, there you are." In terms of this discussion, you can rephrase that: "No matter where you go, your projected mental overlay goes with you." For this simple reason, growth as a lucid dreamer naturally involves self-examination and inquiry. In almost all cases, you cannot escape yourself. Your projected mental overlay radiates around you, invisibly touching your experience.

How to Project Your Belief

In a lucid dream, look around for something that seems positively connected to movement (skateboard, wagon, car, plane, bicycle). Knowingly transfer onto the selected dream object your belief in its power to move you around the dreamscape. Invest it with the power of movement. Then hold onto it and let it take you to places that you wish to go. What happens?

If you really want to challenge yourself for extra credit, try projecting your belief onto an inappropriate symbol of movement like a ship's anchor, a giant boulder, or a large skyscraper. Knowingly transfer onto it your belief in its power to move you around the dreamscape. Invest it with the power of movement. Then hold on. What happens? If you can get a skyscraper like the Empire State Building to flit around the dreamscape as easily as a magic broom, then you have truly mastered the idea of projecting the power of belief into an object. Congratulations!

Psychology and the Pygmalion Effect

Psychology has studied the power of belief and expectations, known as the Pygmalion Effect, in numerous real-world settings. A classic example of the Pygmalion Effect occurred in an elementary-school research study, in which researchers told teachers that a new test confirmed that certain students seemed prepared to spurt ahead in their learning. In actuality, the students had been selected at random and seemed no better or worse than average in learning potential.

The result? In the classes where teachers believed certain students were prepared to move forward, those students showed a statistically significant increase in their test scores when compared to others in their class and the control group. Apparently, the teachers' belief and expectation in the students' ability to spurt ahead created an environment in which that became achievable.[54]

Opposite to the Pygmalion Effect, the Golem Effect suggests that low expectations normally lead to a noticeable decrease in performance. Commonly, we refer to these effects as self-fulfilling prophesies in which we consciously or subconsciously help create what we already believe and expect. Because of the pervasive nature and power of our expectations, science has sought to avoid this type of bias in scientific experiments by using double-blind studies and similar safeguards whenever possible.

Whether waking, dreaming, or even lucid dreaming, it appears that your beliefs and expectations project outward and mentally overlay your experience. In lucid dreaming, you can see this easily, because a change in belief and expectation almost instantly becomes manifest. Knowing this about the subconscious should make you even more aware of your waking beliefs and expectations, and encourage you to examine your mind actively and let go of your unproductive, limiting beliefs and expectations.

As a lucid dreamer, you can play around with the whole set of physically based efforts: swimming through dreamspace, flapping your arms like a bird, or running to begin gliding. You can manipulate your mind and actively project the power of belief onto an appropriate item symbolically connected to flight and use that power of belief to propel you through the lucid dream. Although this can teach you important lessons in lucidity, there are even more advanced ways of moving successfully through inner space that you can try.

Advanced Movement Techniques

According to science, our physical universe consists of about 95 percent dark matter (of which we have no examples) and dark energy. Of the remaining 5 percent, most consists of plasma or highly ionized gas emitted from places like our sun. When it gets down to what we think of as physical objects, these amount to less than 1 percent of the total. Curiously, we spend a lot of time focused on that 1 percent and little time considering the vastness of space.

As you progress in lucid dreaming, dealing with space will require more of your attention. When you want to fly across a vast field to a faraway castle in your lucid dream, how can you manage that without exhausting yourself by flapping your arms? In a small room, it may make sense to walk or swim over to your friend in your lucid dream, but in a vast open area, where you see a castle that you want to explore, this may be problematic. Here are some ways to deal with the issue.

Concentrating Your Focus with Intent

When you want to travel across vast distances in your dream, I suggest using a three-part technique called "concentrated focus with intent."

Using this technique requires you to remember and practice three simple steps:

- While you are aware in a lucid dream, concentrate on the place you want to be.

- Focus deeply on that place by feeling it, imagining yourself touching it, or engaging your perception with that specific place.

- Now that you have concentrated your focus, let go and intend yourself there.

You can practice this kind of active imagination while awake as well. As you go about your day, look around. When you see an appropriate place—the top of a telephone pole, a small ledge on a skyscraper, or the dome of a church—recall the three-step process of concentrated focus with intent. Concentrate on the exact place you want to be, imagine yourself touching it or engaging it, and then let go by intending yourself there. When you do this during the day, you learn the practice and feel of it, which makes it easy to perform in your next lucid dream.

How to Concentrate Your Focus

In your mind's eye imagine that you are lucid. Hundreds of meters away, you see a castle with a golden turret and a fluttering blue flag on top. Can you see it? Now concentrate on that flagstaff. Using your mind, sense it or feel it and then simply let go and intend yourself to it. Normally, you will find yourself magically flying toward it with ease and grace. In mere seconds, you will stand on the turret, holding the flagstaff, and look back triumphantly at the distance you covered.

When using this method to mentally manipulate dream space, you do not consider the mechanics of how to get there. You simply concentrate your focus on where you want to be, imaginatively sense it, and then let go. Your concentrated focus and your intent provide all the necessary energy to take you there naturally. Using this technique, you see how mental principles work to move your awareness through inner space with relative ease.

In this lucid dream from August 2002, I use this basic idea of concentrated focus with intent:

> I tell my friend: "Let's fly! I'll show you how." I grab her arm and we fly about fifty feet. We do this a few more times, going about fifty feet. She gets better each time.
>
> I finally tell her that to fly easily when lucid, you have to "see yourself where you want to be." I point to a car far away and say: "See yourself there and then fly; it's easier." I joke with her and we laugh about it. We easily fly there. We go past a gate and into a beautiful garden. It is like a mini-paradise.

Reading the lucid dreams of experienced lucid dreamers can bring you new and fascinating ideas that might never have occurred to you. Seeing how they act and the rationale behind their actions often expands your own belief system or enhances your willingness to experiment with new concepts. Besides your personal limiting beliefs, you may find that you have adopted cultural and even scientifically based limiting beliefs. As the humorist Mark Twain observed in his book *Innocents Abroad*: "Travel is fatal to prejudice, bigotry, and narrow-mindedness, and many of our people need it sorely on these accounts." For this reason, it seems wise to travel widely in lucid dreams and see the relative nature of your belief system tested.

Manipulating Dream Space

Experienced lucid dreamers have discussed other ways of moving within their lucid dreams. Beverly D'Urso, who took part in many of LaBerge's lucid dream experiments, recalls that she began to play with the idea of space in her lucid dreams. For example, instead of trying to fly to far-off places like Paris, she firmly intended to discover the Eiffel Tower behind her when she turned around in her dream. She notes that this technique worked quite well for her. After a while, however, she missed the journeying aspect of moving through space.

On another occasion, Beverly reports that she became lucid and recalled her intent to meet a friend in the Bahamas while dreaming. Lucid, she considered how to get there and realized that flying would take too long. Then she decided to place her awareness into a nearby phone line and use it as a conduit to her destination, thinking: "I could make myself miniature, go into the wire as electricity itself, and get there very quickly."[55] She felt her awareness whooshing through the phone line, like little electrons through a cable. She eventually popped out in a Caribbean setting, lucidly aware.

Alan Worsley, the British lucid dreamer who first signaled his lucid awareness in Keith Hearne's sleep lab in 1975, wrote about his investigation into manipulating space. Instead of him deciding to fly to a place on the dream horizon, he simply willed the place to come to him and watched as it did so.[56] He realized that the dream object or environment had no fundamental stationary position.

Worsley apparently acted from the perspective that lucid dreaming space existed in his mind, so instead of using any physical effort or investing in any physical movement, he simply manipulated the *idea* of space. Considering mental space makes you wonder what *near* and *far* actually mean in lucid dreams. What separates two objects in the inner space of lucid dreaming?

Some lucid dreamers have also used another version of projecting belief onto a dream object to move through space by creating a lucid dream portal. For example, they may believe that stepping into a mirror can act as a portal to move to another place. When lucid, they step into a mirror, firmly intending to travel to Japan. Once through the mirror, they normally find themselves in a Japanese setting.

Other lucid dreamers approach this differently. They look at the mirror's reflection until they see the place they wish to be and then jump into the mirror and find themselves at that place. If, looking into the mirror, they see the onion domes of Red Square in Moscow, they simply jump in at that moment and suddenly find themselves there. In essence, the mirror acts as a reflection of the accessibility of another dream space or another mental place. The use of mirrors by lucid dreamers has become so fascinating that *Lucid Dreaming Experience* featured an entire issue on it.[57]

Occasionally, lucid dreamers encounter a wormhole or portal that naturally exists in a lucid dream. Stepping into it often leads to moving through a tunnel of light and then popping into a new dream or a new lucid dream environment. I have had knowledgeable dream figures show me that, if I move my awareness into a certain space or place in a lucid dream—usually to my immediate right—I will enter a new dream or new lucid dreamscape. When I do this, I often encounter a wormhole effect of moving through a tunnel of light until finally emerging into a completely new dream.

Lucid dreamer Linda Mastrangelo presented a paper on moving through portals, appropriately titled "Alice's Looking Glass: Exploring Portals in Other Dimensions in Lucid Dreams." She wrote about her unique experience:

> Surprisingly over time, I discovered that right before I became lucid, a portal or opening would appear in my periphery usually to the right of me, so before bedtime, I would tell myself repeatedly and specifically that I will become lucid by looking to the right for a portal. I even practiced somatically by moving my eyes physically to the right with great results.[58]

Like Alice in Wonderland, Mastrangelo discovered that lucid dream portals act as powerful "looking glasses" to enter new dream spaces.

During these events, lucid dreaming offers an expanded sense of space, showing you the nature of intra-dream space plus dimensional movement—or perhaps even multidimensional movement, when you leave one dimension and then find yourself in another. Sometimes, the act of waking from one of these lucid experiences conveys the sense that even the movement from dreaming to waking involves a movement of awareness across dimensions. Perhaps modern physicists may someday explore theories about the nature of reality through experimenting with dimensions and mental space in lucid dreams.

Playing Mind Games

In the mental space of lucid dreams, using mental actions (belief, expectation, focus, intent, and *will*) seems much more appropriate and successful than using physical actions. If you find yourself using physical actions in the mental space of lucid dreams, you apparently believe that physical action seems the most appropriate choice. If so, your projected mental overlay may be blinding you to the other possible methods of mental manipulation. Knowing this, in the following lucid dream scenarios, circle *P* if the response imitates physical action; circle *M* if it shows largely mental actions.

> **Dream 1:** When I realize that I do not live in San Francisco, I become lucid and look around, marveling at the detail and color of this lucid dream! I notice the Golden Gate Bridge about a mile away and decide to fly to the top. At that moment, I begin to:
>
> • Run as fast as I can, so I have enough speed to glide there. (M or P)
>
> • Realize that I need to focus on the top and intend myself there. (M or P)
>
> • Swim through the air, using the breaststroke. (M or P)
>
> • Act on the assumption that the entire scene exists as a creation of my mind, so I use my will to bring the Golden Gate Bridge to me. (M or P)
>
> **Dream 2:** Lucidly aware, I decide to investigate a strange mansion. I come to a door and open it, but see only a thick brick wall. At that moment, I want to get past it, so I decide to:
>
> • Look around for a hammer and smash the brick wall. (M or P)

- Realize that the wall exists as dream stuff and walk through it. (M or P)

- Announce to the dream that, when I close the door, the brick wall will disappear. (M or P)

- Get a couple of strong guys to help me push over the brick wall. (M or P)

Dream 3: I see my grandmother; I know she died ten years ago, so this must be a dream. Lucid, I wonder whether I can heal the arthritis in my knees. At that moment, I decide to:

- Seek a dream doctor to give me a pill or write a prescription. (M or P)

- Create a ball of healing light and place it over each knee. (M or P)

- Ask my grandmother whether she knows any home remedies for arthritis. (M or P)

- Focus on my knees while saying: "Now from my hands with power divine, the healing light on my knees will shine!"(M or P)

Look over your responses. Do you see how imitating physical actions may work but require lots of effort when compared to using mental actions?

In lucid dreaming, you have unlimited choices, theoretically. However, you normally act in accordance with your assumptions or projected mental overlay. Thankfully, your beliefs, feelings, and expectations can change—and change in an instant—so that you realize your inherent freedom and power can affect your experience. When you take time to conduct a post-lucid dream debriefing, look at how you respond to the dream events.

Movement and the Expectation Effect

Sometimes your beliefs adjust to a given situation and, at that moment, you see that your expectation about the situation largely determines your experience. For example, you believe that you are of average height, but when placed on a bus with a professional basketball team, how do you expect to feel? Of course, most of you expect to feel short in that instance, maybe even tiny.

I call this sudden situational change in our normal beliefs the "expectation effect." My classic lucid dream example involves flying through a wall with ease because I see it as nothing more than projected mental energy. However, minutes later, I decide to fly back through it, but notice how substantial and concrete the wall looks from the other side. Suddenly, I expect a bit of trouble. Yes, the lucid dream mirrors my concern precisely, as I get stuck half in and half out of the wall. After a few seconds, I tell myself this seems ridiculous and push through the wall easily.

The expectation effect suggests that *you get what you expect to the degree that you expect it at that exact moment.* Many lessons in lucidity involve managing your expectations. If you expect the hostess to act seductively, then, suddenly, she plays the role of temptress. If you expect the traffic officer to hassle you, he suddenly wants to see your identification. Knowing this, you can flip your expectations to something more positive.

How to Flip the Expectation Effect

Play with the expectation effect in your next lucid dream. Whenever you find yourself in a situation that activates your expectations, use the expectation effect to change the typical, expected outcome. If you see a baby in a crib, flip your normal expectations and expect the baby to discuss politics, the economy, or higher mathematics. If you see an old friend, flip your common expectation about your friend's personality and expect the person to act differently. If you see a miserly person on the street, flip your normal expectation and expect him to have money to offer you.

By playing with your beliefs, expectations, and other mental processes, you begin to understand their importance in co-creating your experience, both in dreaming and in waking. That knowledge can help you become more awake and more aware in your day-to-day existence and learn to live more lucidly.

Focusing Your Attention

Let's say you find yourself in London, coming up out of the Tube station at Piccadilly Circus. When you get to the surface, on what do you focus?

Well, it depends. A hungry person may focus on restaurants. A tourist may focus on the flashing lights of the theaters. A businessman may focus on the *Financial Times* in the window of a news shop. A child may focus on the pigeons.

In lucid dreaming, your focus helps determine your experience and how you relate to the space around you. Moreover, it helps select where your energy goes in that space. It may emerge as a type of habit, as need, or as personal values; but no matter what internal compass you use, you will likely go in the direction of your focus.

You saw the importance of focus when flying and moving within inner space. Focusing on your goal will likely get you there. If you focus on the ground or on your fear of hitting the ground, you will likely crash. If you focus on the castle turret, your focus will likely move you there with ease. Where your focus goes, there too goes your energy. So pay attention and focus on where you want to end up!

Focus also has levels of perspective in lucid dreaming. Beginners usually focus on the obvious and apparent things around them. Intermediate lucid dreamers may focus on those obvious and apparent things plus what they imply (Piccadilly Circus implies the sights of London, like Buckingham Palace). Experienced lucid dreamers may focus beyond the obvious and the implied and go instead to the vast infinite potential of lucid dreaming. You can see how experienced lucid dreamers learn to use focus more broadly and not feel constrained so much by their perceived environment.

Although your immediate interest may determine why you focus on a specific thing, some scientific research suggests that your cultural socialization and belief system subtly influence how you focus and relate to the objects within space as well. In the book *The Geography of Thought: How*

Asians and Westerners Think Differently . . . And Why, Richard Nesbitt reports on various research studies showing differences in how Asians and Westerners perceive and process an experience like seeing a painting for the first time. By using eye-tracking technology and detailed questionnaires, Nesbitt identified distinct cultural differences as the two groups focused on a painting. Westerners tended to focus more on the primary object and largely ignored the background, whereas Asians viewed the work more holistically and noticed how the background provided a context for the various objects in the foreground.[59]

Insights like this suggest that even cultural upbringing and socialization may play an unseen role in how lucid dreamers relate to the contents of their dreams. Beneath the surface level of their projected mental overlay, they see that deeper, culturally ingrained aspects actually influence how they perceive and relate to the world around them.

As you play around with space in lucid dreams, you may note that it serves a dual function. Space separates objects and externalizes them from you and from each other. But space also allows an infinite number of relationships to exist between you and objects, and between the objects themselves. Space seems almost mathematical when viewed like this.

How to Focus on Space

In one of your upcoming lucid dreams, try turning away from your focus on objects and begin to focus solely on space. Lucidly run down the hallway in your dream and open every door. Does this help in creating space? Look more and more closely at an item to see its ultimate depth. Can you get beyond the surface to deeper and deeper levels? See what the final frontier of space can teach you as you playfully move through, expand, and collapse dream space.

Reality and the Structure of Experience

In this chapter, we have focused on many important issues related to moving through and manipulating dream space. For many of us, the difficulty involves letting go of the tendency to project physical ideas of movement and manipulation (swimming through space, flapping arms, running, and so on) onto a mental environment. This type of unexamined projected mental overlay can frustrate beginners, until they realize that the solution exists in their belief systems and minds, not out there in their lucid dreams.

As you develop your lucid dreaming skills, you actually become more aware of unexamined and tacit assumptions, feelings, and beliefs (that is, your inner mental overlay). Lucid dreaming helps you wake up to the power of beliefs, expectations, and intent in their dual roles as both revealers and concealers of the fundamental nature of things. Moreover, it makes evident that your own personal limiting beliefs—both waking and dreaming—can constrain you from living life more fully.

The reality-creating principles of belief, expectation, and focus have received some attention in this chapter. In later chapters, we will look at the reality-creating principles of intent and *will* and their role in helping to create experience and show us the larger reality of our awareness.

Chapter 6

DREAM OBJECTS AND SETTINGS

Social psychologist Kurt Lewin has observed: "If you want truly to understand something, try to change it." When you begin to change something in a system (your family, your school, your business, your neighborhood), the entire system responds and reveals previously unnoticed connections, relationships, and associations. By observing that change, a careful observer gains insight into the dynamic nature of the underlying system and how it actually works.

Because lucid dreaming allows for conscious deliberation and experimentation, you can literally change almost any aspect of a lucid dream. Can you stop the dream action or even rewind the dream? Can you remove the color from the dream scene? As you try to change it, you see how the underlying system or matrix of dreaming responds and you move closer to Lewin's goal of deeper understanding.

During their formal training in the philosophy and practice of dream yoga, Buddhist students get basic instruction in lucid dreaming. Once lucid, students in some traditions, like the Dzogchen, are encouraged by the teacher to alter categories of experience. By altering or changing the lucid dream experience, they develop a deeper understanding of how their mental actions affect their experience in the realm of dreaming. In the Buddhist dream yoga tradition, the goal is to use philosophical insights, various practices, and lucid dream realizations in pursuit of eventual enlightenment. Practices like how to change categories of experience focus on educating practitioners about the mind's role in co-creating experience so that a more insightful understanding of the nature of mind occurs.

By contrast, Western lucid dreamers with a different interest and philosophy may use similar practices for other purposes. Consider Gestalt psychologist Paul Tholey's observations about moderating speed in a lucid dream. He realized that this ability could have applications in the physical world as well, like helping athletes learn new skills and become comfortable with new settings. For example, an internationally successful equestrian, Sladko Solinski, wrote to Tholey and explained how he used lucid dreaming to prepare for equestrian competitions. Riding the upcoming course on his horse in a lucid dream, he determines the exact figures to make.

> I manage to do this in slow motion, giving the horse assistance at exactly the right moment in a particular movement phase. During lucid dreaming, I ride the course through several times (three to nine times), *exactly and completely.* [emphasis added] Based on this experience, my body knowledge is sufficient to get through the course autonomously, that is, without conscious or deliberate effort.[60]

Tholey concluded that the ability to manipulate speed in a lucid dream offers major advantages to athletes and competitors. They can practice in slow motion and gain extra body awareness to perform better in the waking world.

Although this practical use of lucid dreaming exists, it also shows the importance of the larger focus, framework, or philosophy of the practitioner. One person may use these lucid skills to excel at a higher level in a sport, whereas another may use them to seek spiritual insight. Fundamentally, your focus in the lucid dreaming practice will decide how the insights are used.

Dream yoga practices can also help lucid dreamers understand that objects (or projected mental energy) have a connection to a dreamer's awareness or mindstream. However, to manipulate a dream object or to enhance physical skills does not seem the primary goal of the dream yoga approach. Rather, dream yoga practitioners seek to realize the mind's projective nature and follow a pathway to transcend it.

How to Change Categories of Experience

In this practice, we consider only the first four categories to change when consciously aware in a dream state: size, quantity, quality, and speed. To read all eleven categories, please see *The Tibetan Yogas of Dream and Sleep* by Tenzin Wangyal Rinpoche.[61]

Size (increase and decrease): When lucid, act to change the size of an object or experience. Can you make a doll's house become as big as a museum? Can you make a Boeing 747 shrink down to the size of a butterfly?

Quantity (multiply and diminish): If you see one object, like a rose, lucidly make it two, three, four, or dozens more. In a lucid dream, if you see many items—like a forest of trees—can you diminish the number and turn 1,000 trees into ten or even a solitary tree?

Quality: When you experience a certain quality or emotion in a lucid dream, stop and transform it. Can you turn a piece of hard steel into a limp, noodle-like bit of metal? When you see something that normally makes you angry, can you transform your feeling into compassion and understanding?

Speed: In lucid dreaming, you can speed things up or slow them down. Practice adjusting speed in your dream. For example, can you wave your hand and put the lucid dream into slow motion? Can you fast-forward a dream? See the flexible nature of experience when you use your mind and attention properly in a lucid dream.

For many beginners, it may seem easier in a lucid dream to walk up to an object, grab it, and stretch it until it becomes huge. On one level, beginners recognize objects as illusory, but may feel they must manipulate them through physical actions. Intermediate lucid dreamers may have the presence of mind to understand that manipulating mental energy through mental practices seems most appropriate in this dimension, so they may mentally grab the corner of an object and stretch it.

Yet even for experienced lucid dreamers, altering dream objects sometimes takes a bit of effort. In an interview with lucid dreamer Joy Fatooh for *Lucid Dream Exchange* magazine, she mentions the Buddhist practice of seeing dream objects as illusory and changing them in a lucid dream:

> But even within a dream, I can't always just think a thought and make it be so. I sometimes have to trick myself past the apparent solidity of the illusion. For instance, once I saw a purple flower in a vase and decided to multiply it. It was stubborn, but I started jumping up and down on the couch like a little kid and seeing another flower appear each time I jumped![62]

Using Lewin's observation that if you want to understand something you should try to change it, notice that, when Joy sought to multiply the number of flowers in the vase, she learned that her focused intent mixed with a little emotion accelerated the multiplication of flowers. More explicitly, her consciousness initiated the process of transforming mental energy into formed objects (new flowers), and she accelerated the process through adding emotion.

Although Joy can see the connection between her conscious activity and the flowers' creation, you may wonder about the appearance of forms or objects outside of a lucid dreamer's conscious intent. For example, when a lucid dreamer flies through a wall and sees a castle and a white horse on the other side, who or what called forth the appearance of the castle and the white horse? More broadly, you may wonder how almost *all* the dream forms, objects, and settings occur in your own dreams. Does your awareness create them? Does your unconscious create them? Or something else? Who or what creates these dream objects?

The Persistent Brick Wall

When you become lucidly aware and touch a nearby brick wall, you can often feel its cool, nubby texture. Although it looks like brick and feels like brick, your lucid awareness should help you realize its actual nature. In essence, the brick wall exists as some type of *formed* mental energy or projected thought, and if you walk through it or put your hand through it, you get evidence for that point.

By understanding the brick wall as projected mental energy, lucid dreamers can often manipulate it more easily and relate to it more thoughtfully. For example, you can create a giant fist and knock away the brick wall. But what if a new brick wall appears in its place and with extra emotion you knock this one away, whereupon an even bigger brick wall appears? What, then, can we say about this piece of projected mental energy?

A beginning lucid dreamer told me a similar story of encountering a persistently reappearing brick wall. As I recall, she noticed something strange and became lucid. Then, just as she meant to move forward in the lucid dream, a massive brick wall suddenly appeared in front of her, blocking her progress. She also realized that she carried a very heavy backpack, which slowed her down as well. Each time she worked to get beyond the massive brick wall, a new brick wall appeared and blocked her progress. She asked a simple question: "Why did this happen to me?"

Although a reappearing brick wall may be frustrating, this example illustrates the depth and complexity of lucid dreaming. Lucid dreamers do not control their lucid dreams so much as they relate to a larger field of awareness—which, in this case, keeps presenting brick walls to the dreamer. Although you can see the brick wall as projected mental energy, you still must relate to it. And when it appears and reappears, you have to wonder who or what projects this mental energy that now stands in your way.

After listening to this lucid dreamer's experience, it seemed to me that some message existed here. Because the brick wall appeared at the moment she wished to move forward, it apparently represented a symbolically expressed barrier in the lucid dream. Perhaps the heavy backpack represented something as well—like her heavy concerns.

Obviously, these dream symbols had meaning specific to this dreamer, and we can only guess at their meaning. In general, however, she reports feeling blocked in her lucid dream (which seems very unusual for most lucid dreamers, who feel utter freedom and joy). Moreover, she is carrying a heavy weight on her back (which again seems unusual for lucid dreamers, who normally report no sense of weight).

In these instances, an experienced lucid dreamer may realize a number of things:

- The brick wall exists as projected mental energy.

- The brick wall also apparently exists as a symbol or piece of information.

- The wall's appearance suggests a deeper significance, requiring a more thoughtful response.

- The wall will likely dissolve once the lucid dreamer makes an *appropriate response*, because the issue (or mental-energy equation) will have changed.

Here, we see the possible value of understanding dreams and dream symbolism, and the engagement with a larger field of awareness. If you realize that your lucid dreaming progress faces a brick wall and consider what that symbolically suggests, you will likely learn something important. And if you realize you are carrying heavy concerns on your back and consider what that may mean, you increase your chance of dealing with that issue. However, if you fail to see the dream symbolism or understand its likely meaning, you are likely to struggle with this symbolic communication in the lucid dream. In all likelihood, another dream will arise in the coming nights, and the information will appear in new or similar symbols and express the issues again as they seek resolution—possibly concerns about lucid dreaming, which lead to blocked movement and expression.

Having some understanding of dream symbolism seems a very important skill for those on the lucid dreaming path. Although many approaches to dream interpretation exist, I have found the books by several authors—including Gayle Delaney (*All About Dreams*),

Patricia Garfield (*The Universal Dream Key*), Teresa DeCicco (*The Giant Compass*), and Justina Lasley (*Honoring the Dream*)—to provide valuable insights.

Each of these authors tends to agree that the specific meaning of a dream symbol seems unique to the dreamer. Although many in the same culture may associate certain meanings with certain symbols, each person's dream symbols have a unique relationship to his or her life experience. For example, a sailboat in a dream may represent adventure or freedom to admirers of sailing, but if you have survived a sailboat sinking in waking life or don't know how to swim, the dream symbol of a sailboat may have a completely different meaning. At the end of this chapter, we include a quick process that author Justina Lasley teaches to help dreamers get more insight into their dream symbols.

Lucid dreaming does offer some advantages in dealing with dream objects, because more fully aware lucid dreamers may notice a brick wall and consider numerous creative responses to it. For example, they may consider its reappearance and ask: "Hey brick wall, what do you represent?" Possibly, they may then hear a response like: "Impediments to progress." Or they may receive a clue about an underlying issue. They may ask: "Brick wall, what must I understand to move beyond you?" Here again, they may hear or see a literal or figurative response like an image of complete trust. Upon waking, they may truly "get it" and realize the necessary changes they must make to their beliefs or emotions.

An example of "getting it" occurred to a woman who had recurring nightmares of being chased by three women. Her therapist gave her instructions on how to become lucidly aware and encouraged her to face the three women and learn something from them. She became lucid one night when she realized that the chase only occurred in the dream state. She indignantly turned to the three women, demanding to know: "Who are you? Why are you chasing me?" The three women responded: "We are your anxieties. You call us to you." When she awoke, she understood her need to work on truly resolving and letting go of her anxiety.

In these lucid dream question-and-answer situations, you can see the conscious mind actively engaging the unconscious awareness and often coming to a new, more constructive understanding. This also happens in regular dreams, although it may take much longer for the ego (the waking self) to comprehend the symbols or issue and make an appropriate response.

In his writings, Carl Jung called the process of the conscious mind coming to terms with the unconscious and successfully resolving opposing tendencies toward a new understanding the "transcendent function." In some lucid dreams, you can see the transcendent function actively achieved as dreamers meet a difficult or oppositional situation and seek to understand what the unconscious offers. Finally, they comprehend, make an appropriate response, and resolve the issue within the dream (or upon waking).

It seems interesting that PTSD sufferers who become lucidly aware just once often report an immediate cessation of their recurring nightmares. In these cases, it appears that the unconscious recognizes the lucid awareness as an appropriate response to the nightmarish projections. After the unconscious receives an appropriate response, it ends the nightly test. The act of lucid awareness seems to satisfy an inner requirement and concludes the need for the nightmare to recur—perhaps as a computer form awaits the proper response and, when received, moves on to a different screen.

Dream Settings as Projected Mental Energy

When you become lucidly aware, look around at the dream setting or environment. If you accept the basic idea that most dream objects normally exist as projections of mental energy, the setting, environment, or backdrop of your dream suggests a projected psychic atmosphere—or a projected mental or emotional atmosphere, if you prefer.

Consider the quality of light when you become lucid. Does the light seem bright and cheery, or dim and foggy? Does that quality of ambient light relate to your state of mind at that moment? If you could change your mental atmosphere in that moment, how would the setting's light respond?

In another study by Voss et.al., of lucid dreaming in German youth, the lucid dream narrative of a ten-year-old girl provides a fundamental glimpse of how emotional changes within her mind become immediately reflected in the lucid dream setting and atmosphere.[63]

Someone was haunting me, and I was with my girlfriend. The chaser stood before me and wanted to kill me, and then I realized it was only a dream, so I made the person disappear, and then suddenly it wasn't dark anymore. (Narrative 3)

Notice what the girl reports about the quality of light. Apparently, in the frightful portion of the dream when a chaser wants to kill her, the atmosphere seems literally dark. But when she becomes lucid and vanquishes the person, the girl reports that "suddenly it wasn't dark anymore." Without any direct action on the lighting by the girl, the lighting seemed to improve naturally with the removal of the feared object. In effect, as her mood lifted, the lighting in the dream reflected this and increased.

Lucid dreamers often have lucid dreams that occur in night settings with twinkling stars. I had a wonderful lucid dream of joyfully flying at night and seeing a fantastic moon twice as big as normal. So joy can certainly exist in the darkness of night, particularly when the darkness feels appropriate to the situation. For this reason, dream work often takes into account the feeling sense of the dreamer in that setting, because it symbolically suggests the nuance of thought and emotion.

I recall another interesting lucid dream of happily dancing in a graveyard at midnight. Although the graveyard setting seemed odd at first glance, I had a sense of burying old, limiting ideas and becoming free of their restrictive influence. The setting and my response reflected the relief and joy of letting things pass away, which leads to transformation and new life. Thoughtful lucid dreamers will notice recurring settings and consider how they likely connect to their mental or emotional state at that moment. Also, they will notice how the setting and atmosphere suddenly changes, when they change their mental or emotional state.

How to Investigate Dream Settings

Although many lucid dreams occur in unknown settings (places you could not find in your waking reality), you may need to investigate the cultural meanings or personal associations you have with settings known to you. Consider a lucid dream in these cultural settings. What qualities, issues, or emotions do you associate with them?

- Your bank (Does this setting remind you of financial issues?)

- Your elementary school classroom

- The police station

- Your local hospital

- Washington, D.C.

- A white, sandy beach

As you think about each of these settings, realize that you have personal or cultural associations with them. A white, sandy beach may bring up memories of relaxation and fun, whereas your elementary school classroom may call up memories of feeling small and confused. Each known setting likely has extra layers of personal meaning and association, which can give you insight into your dream or lucid dream.

I recall a lucid dream that happened outside of my childhood home near one specific corner of the property. In the dream, I watched someone in a very unfortunate situation and heard him complain about another person. Upon waking, I wondered about this setting. Then I realized that this specific corner of our property served as the location of the annual summer boxing match in my youth. With that realization, the sense of aggression expressed in the dream by one person toward another made this a very appropriate setting.

As you develop your dreaming and lucid dreaming skills, you may notice possible associations with each dream setting and learn what it suggests mentally, emotionally, and symbolically—something I learned to do more thoughtfully by listening to author Nigel Hamilton.[64] After a dream or lucid dream, consider these various questions about the setting:

- Did the setting seem constricted or wide open?

- Did the environment seem bright and colorful, dull, or black-and-white?

- Did the area suggest a sense of value? Did it convey vibrant growth or activity? Was it boring or bland? Was it neglected or utterly devastated?

- Did the setting seem hospitable or supportive of your development? What movements did you make in this space?

- Was any change in your thinking, feeling, or acting reflected in the scene? For example, you become lucid and realize how you can escape the room with no doors and now find yourself in a spacious, grand setting.

When you consider the setting or settings within a lucid dream, you may get a broad perspective on the dream's overall emotional sense or symbolic commentary. Because innumerable settings exist, these questions may not seem appropriate to all your lucid dreams. Nonetheless, dream settings normally contain some meaning or provide a sense of context for the dream.

Dream Mapping

Some lucid dreamers use a dream's setting as a clue to help them become lucid. How? By beginning to focus on their location in waking life and in their dreaming life through a process called "dream mapping."

Many times throughout the day, these dreamers encourage a lucid mindset (see chapter 3) by asking: "Where am I now? How did I get here?" Then they actively examine the setting and their path there to determine whether it seems to be a dream setting or a waking place. At night, this line of personal examination naturally carries over into a dream, whereupon they then ask the critical question: "Where am I now? How did I get here?" This critical review sometimes prompts lucidity, as they realize they cannot explain how they arrived there and wonder whether they are dreaming.

The idea of dream mapping, as explained in an IASD presentation[65] by a lucid dreamer from the Ukraine, takes a page from the shamanic tradition of mapping out shamanic journeys and inner realms. These lucid dreamers create an actual physical map (on a grid) of each night's dream locale, relative to the sensed location of their home in the dream (home serving as the center point of the grid).

On waking, these dreamers recall the setting—for example, an industrial area—realize that it seemed southeast of their home, and mark it on their map. As the dream mapping continues, they find themselves becoming lucid when they return to places they have been to before in other dreams and recall that they exist as locations in a dream. Therefore, they must be dreaming now. In dream mapping, the location acts as a prompt for lucid awareness. In addition, sometimes active dream mappers find themselves in a new setting, which may encourage them to examine critically how they got there. Thinking about that often leads them to become lucid.

After many months or even years of dream mapping, the dream state begins to take on a very concrete existence. In fact, during lucid dreams, dream mappers can recall their dream map and move to places where special items (like wormholes) or powerful dream figures have appeared in previous lucid dreams. Curiously, they sometimes even compare notes and find that their personal dream maps often have striking areas of correspondence with those of other dream mappers (e.g., the industrial area shows up in the southeast quadrant of many maps). By focusing on location, these dreamers learn how to map their inner space, and how to use that map to get lucid.

For those of us who have never made a dream map, we can still become lucid simply by noticing the surrounding area. The following examples show settings that have encouraged me to become lucid:

- Sitting at an elementary school desk helped me realize I had graduated from college and no longer attended school; I became lucid.

- Easily getting up from a red dirt playground struck me as strange; I became lucid.

- Seeing snow on the ground made me wonder about the date, and I recalled it was the middle of May; I became lucid.

- In my old hometown, I saw a parking lot where I knew houses stood; I became lucid (although years later, a parking lot did come to exist on that very spot).

Dream Settings as Drama

Some dream workers feel that most dreams come in three basic sections, much like theatrical performances. In the first part, the dream introduces you to the basic issue or conflict. In the middle portion, you experience your response or reaction to the issue or conflict, which can sometimes seem quite involved. Finally, at the dream's end, some sort of resolution occurs (which may or may not be constructive). Viewing a dream as a three-act play may provide some insight into its symbols and the informational or educational nature of the dream.

When you become lucidly aware, settings often provide significant clues about your mental and emotional atmosphere in a broad sense. Unlike dream objects, which contain or represent specific patterns of mental energy, dream settings show you a broad snapshot of the prevailing mental atmosphere. However, like the weather in waking reality, dream settings can change—especially in a lucid dream when *you focus on changing it*—which basically means changing your thoughts or feelings. Seeing dream settings as symbolically expressive of your mental atmosphere may help you see the larger context.

Developing your appreciation of symbols can help you navigate dreams and lucid dreams with greater skill and agility. As you follow the Selecting and Redefining Nouns practice from Justina Lasley's book *Honoring the Dream*[66], you may gain a new sense of the symbolic information hidden in dream objects and settings. Just as the Chinese 梦中变大 script may make no sense to you, for someone trained in that language, it makes perfect sense and conveys important information. As a lucid dreamer, it helps you learn and grow when you grasp the basics of dreaming's frequently symbolic language.

Selecting and Redefining Nouns[67]

This exercise is very powerful in helping the dreamer understand how images represent aspects of himself or of situations in his waking life.

- Ask the dreamer to look back over the written dream and make a vertical list of all the nouns in the dream (down the left side of the page).

- Beside each noun, put three descriptive words or very short phrases. For example, beside *dog*, the dreamer might write, "playful, obedient, unconditional love"; beside *house*, he might write, "where I live, where I feel safe, where I am protected."

- Rewrite the entire dream, using the descriptive words rather than the nouns. (It may be necessary to use a phrase such as "A situation that is," "The part of myself that is," or "A place that is.")

- Encourage the dreamer not to get caught up in "doing it right" but to focus on uncovering meaning and understanding through the exercise.

So, if you had a short dream, "I found myself walking to my office. Right as I came up to it, I watched my dog leave the office and run away," you would replace all the nouns with descriptive words and rewrite the dream.

The rewritten dream might read like this, "I found myself walking to the place where I work and earn money. Right as I came to it, I watched my playful, obedient, unconditional love leave the place where I work and earn money, and run away."

What insights occur to you when you do this with your own dream?

Chapter 7

INTERACTING WITH COMPLEX DREAM FIGURES

I remember the first time actress Kim Cattrall (from the television and movie series *Sex and the City*) smiled at me. Walking up a street, I looked to my left and saw her coming across the road in a bikini. I smiled at her; she smiled at me. A bit star-struck, I began to think of my good fortune at seeing Kim Cattrall in person—and so enticingly attired. Then it hit me: Why would Kim Cattrall come to my town and walk around in a bikini?

By now, you have guessed that, in the next moment, I realized I was dreaming and became completely lucid. I ignored the dream figure of Kim Cattrall and flew up the street, lucidly aware.

In a commonly held cultural view, dream figures normally represent some aspect of yourself projected outward for you to engage in the dream. Others may add that dream figures exist as archetypes or as unconscious patterns or images that exemplify certain inherent qualities. For example, Kim Cattrall may represent sensuality or femininity or some other archetypal quality. In the cultural view, my awareness in the dream engages this dream symbol (or projected part of me) to become aware of information, resolve emotional issues, or adjust to changing life circumstances.

You can find evidence to support this commonly held cultural view in some lucid dreams, such as this one from April 2005:

> I find myself and my oldest brother at a kitchen table in an old farmhouse in the South. As the homemaker puts beans

on my plate, she looks disapprovingly at someone behind me. I turn and see a tall attractive black woman standing there. This seems a bit strange, so I look at my brother again and realize I am dreaming this.

Aware now, I stand up and want to know what this means. Lucid, I pick up the black woman and place her in front of me, asking: "Who are you? Who are you?" She looks at me and surprises me with her unexpected response: "I am a discarded aspect of yourself." I sense the truth of this and think of how to respond, and then I decide to accept her completely. As I mentally accept her, she suddenly collapses into wisps of colored light, which then enter my torso and give me a jolt of energy. She seems to evaporate into me as a brief wisp of light energy.[67]

In this example, I struggle a bit to determine the proper response to this projected self aspect and then decide complete and loving acceptance seems most appropriate. I felt different upon waking, and it took me about a week to realize how. As it turned out, each day after that dream, I began to think that I should try to write a book on lucid dreaming, even though I had tried a few years earlier and given up. But now, surprisingly, I suddenly felt the energy and confidence to do so. This led to my first book, *Lucid Dreaming: Gateway to the Inner Self.*

When lucidly aware, you have unique capabilities when you engage dream figures. A lucid dreamer has the ability to do the following:

- Converse with a dream figure and hear what it has to say.

- Question a dream figure and see how it responds.

- Respond to a figure's information more thoughtfully.

- Engage a dream figure in many activities, like flying, solving problems, and more.

- Project their own feelings directly onto a dream figure.

- Completely ignore a dream figure and do something else.

For some, the lucid dream I describe above may serve as an exemplar of the Jungian idea of individuation or psychological integration, in which a person becomes aware of disconnected portions of the self and seeks to integrate them into a more complete, whole personality or Self. Often, this involves becoming more conscious of the normally unconscious portions of one's identity and integrating those energies.

When I saw the woman standing behind me, I also realized that she stood in the shadow's position—behind me. Jung felt that the ignored, denied, or repressed aspects of the self (the shadow) often literally took up a position behind the person. Seeing this gave me a hint in the lucid dream that something needed attention, thus my question to establish her identity.

Lucid dreaming seems a promising tool for self-integration, because greater awareness offers the opportunity to engage portions of the unconscious more thoughtfully and with constructive healing intent. However, it may take science some time to fathom the complex nature of dream figures and, in turn, to accept and understand the process of integration. Thankfully, lucid dreaming can help with that endeavor.

The Abilities of Dream Figures

In 1989, German researcher Paul Tholey published a paper titled "Consciousness and Abilities of Dream Characters Observed during Lucid Dreaming."[68] In it, he reports the results of several phenomenological experiments in which nine male, experienced lucid dreamers interacted with dream figures, asking them to draw, write, make rhyming words, create verses, and solve arithmetic problems. The results from ninety-two lucid dreams showed that some dream figures agreed to do the tasks and did them successfully for the most part—oddly enough, performing poorly in arithmetic tasks when the answer exceeded twenty.

Tholey begins his paper with these observations:

> In lucid dreams, dream characters sometimes give the impression of having consciousness of their own. They speak and behave logically, perform amazing cognitive feats, and express in their behavior distinct purposes and feelings, but do they have a consciousness of their own?

By virtue of his experiments, Tholey felt that, when using lucid dreams in therapy, "communication with dream characters should be handled as if they were rational beings."

More recent research on the abilities of dream figures has occurred in Germany. Researchers Tadas Stumbrys, Daniel Erlacher, and Steffen Schmidt provided mathematical tasks to male and female lucid dreamers and urged them to have dream figures perform them in lucid dreams. They report: "Only a third of their answers were correct. . . . Surprisingly, dream characters were more successful with multiplication and division tasks than with addition and subtraction."[69] Some dream figures refused to do the tests when asked, and one dream figure even started to cry. The researchers also noted:

> One participant reported that he kept on doing the experiment [after the experimental period ended] and had an impression that dream characters tended to provide more correct answers after he had repeated the experiment in several lucid dreams.

In a similar study, "An Exploratory Study of Creative Problem Solving in Lucid Dreams: Preliminary Findings and Methodological Considerations," Stumbrys, along with Michael Daniels, found that dream figures tend to do better with solving creative problems and have more trouble with logic problems.[70] Although the commonly held cultural view sees dream figures as mere symbols, the experience of many lucid dreamers urges science to explore their complex nature even more thoughtfully.

Deeper research may conclude that dream figures actually vary in their awareness, behavior, and conversational ability. Numerous lucid dreamers report that some dream figures dislike or protest at being called "dream figures" or "dream characters." Consider this example sent to me by lucid dreamer Robert Hoss, author of *Dream Language: Self Understanding through Imagery and Color*. He becomes lucidly aware and then asks his inner awareness: "Show me something I need to know."

The lucid dream sparked into white light, and I found myself in a lecture hall teaching a class on lucid dreaming to about 20 dream characters. It was a back and forth discussion between the class and me about interactions within a dream and what it was like to be a dream character. It felt like I had been lecturing for 45 minutes.

At one point, a girl in the class raised her hand and said, "Wait a minute, if I am just a dream character, then how come I can recall a whole life before this moment. I have a husband and children and a whole other life." Since it was an interactive discussion I turned to the class and said, "This is an interesting question; how many of you can remember a life of your own before this moment?" About six dream character students immediately raised their hands. Then, ever so slowly, as each student thought about it, they began to slowly raise their hands until all 20 had done so, recalling a life prior to that moment. I then woke in amazement.

Lucid dreamers often refer to dream figures who behave in this manner as independent agents. You may find that independent agents converse, think, and act in ways that seem utterly unexpected and outside of your conscious mental overlay. These surprising experiences offer you innumerable lessons in lucidity. Consider this short list of possibities:

- Dream figures may appear independent, conscious, and separate from the dreamer.

- Dream figures may act to show that the dreamer does not solely create the dream experience.

- Dream figures may disagree with the dreamer's assessment; for example, they see the dream space as the ultimately real platform of experience.

- Dream figures may respond in a completely creative and unexpected manner, outside of the dreamer's mental models or expectations.

Paul Tholey noted the complex nature of this type of dream figure when he wrote:

> In order to avoid misunderstanding, we can never empirically prove whether or not other dream characters are lucid, only that they speak and behave as if they were. Elsewhere I have argued that many dream figures seem to perform with a consciousness of what they are doing.[71]

Tholey's observations and the numerous lucid dream encounters reported suggest that the commonly accepted view of dream figures as simple symbolic projections fails to account for those figures who are complex and independent, and who have apparent self-consciousness within the dream. Although this set of independent agents may represent only a small percentage of dream figures, their presence shows the need for deeper investigation.

As a lucid dreamer, you may come across certain dream figures (besides actresses like Kim Cattrall) who prompt your lucid awareness. Consider this list of figures whom lucid dreamers have encountered:

- Dream figures who question you about the nature of your current state or experience. These enable your lucid awareness by making you reflect more critically. For example, a dream figure may ask: "When did we last meet?" As you search your mind, you realize you met in last night's dream (and, it is hoped, become lucid upon that realization).

- Dream figures who literally tell you that you dream. Remarkably, some dreamers report dream figures telling them this and, on occasion, acting in such a way as to provide evidence (e.g., they begin floating).

- Dream figures who change their appearance repeatedly. For example, you may watch a dream figure whose clothing changes from queenly robes to a simple dress to undergarments. As you notice this, it strikes you as odd, and you realize that you are dreaming.

- Dream figures who look different. You may dream of a figure with bluish skin or eyes with whirls of color and then realize that you are dreaming.

- Deceased dream figures whom you know personally. Numerous dreamers report becoming lucidly aware when they see someone they realize has passed. Examples exist in which the deceased dream figure conveys previously unknown information to the dreamer.

When dream figures act to catalyze your critical thinking and make you wonder whether you are dreaming, you see how they can play a pivotal role in altering your awareness. Moreover, some dream figures actually seem lucidly aware *before* the dreamer becomes lucid. Tholey noted this strange twist, writing: "We can illustrate this by means of an example in which another dream character not only becomes lucid before the dream-ego [lucid dreamer], he also possesses a higher degree of lucidity than the dream-ego later achieves."[72]

That final point shows the depth and complexity of the inner realm of dreaming. Does the lucid dreamer dream the dream into being if another dream figure seems lucid before the lucid dreamer? What about the lucid dream figure who directs the action while the lucid dreamer observes? In those cases, *who dreams the dream*?

Conversing with Dream Figures

Many beginning lucid dreamers experience little success when conversing with dream figures. In their lucid dreams, questions to dream figures often result in blank stares, cryptic responses, or looks of bewilderment. After a number of one-sided conversations, many beginners come to believe that dream figures have nothing intelligent to say.

Tholey felt that beginning lucid dreamers often fail to understand conversations with dream figures. "Inexperienced lucid dreamers frequently have difficulty conducting a rational dialogue with other dream figures. This is because most of these figures play word games involving hidden or multiple meanings which the dream-ego cannot initially understand." Tholey discovered that the dream figures' responses "can later often be shown to have a logical meaning," although it may seem nonsensical in the lucid dream.[73]

The following guidelines for lucid dreamers should result in more interesting and varied dream conversations:

Ask open-ended questions. Questions like "What do you represent?" or "Who are you?" can lead to interesting exchanges. Do not tell a dream figure that you see it as a dream figure. Perhaps it sees *you* as a dream figure.

Do not insult a dream figure. Do not convey prejudiced assumptions in the form of questions like: "Do you know I am dreaming you?" Most dream figures will just stare at you with disinterest or contempt when you say such things.

Take time to consider the responses. If a verbal response does not make sense, ask the dream figure for clarification. Sometimes a response can come as a change in the setting or dream symbols.

Realize that dream figures vary in awareness. One figure may be much more knowledgeable and conversant than another. Look for dream figures that appear active and alert.

Approach conversations with a sense of openness. Show a desire to learn. Let go of assumptions and see what you experience.

Thought Forms—or Something More?

Paul Tholey realized the possibility of creating dream figures where none existed before. He explains that, in the direct approach, he basically breathes them into life: "For example, when I am angry or afraid in a [lucid] dream, I can blow out the anger or fear through my mouth and thereby create a dream character which takes on an appearance corresponding to the emotion."[74] Here, he essentially expresses his emotion with the expectation of a dream figure, and then a newly formed one appears with those characteristics.

In Tholey's second approach, he relies on acting in a way that triggers a strong emotional expectation that calls forth some unconscious response. He provides an example of his approach in this lucid dream:

I knocked down a dream figure in an enclosed room in order to see if I would be punished. I was seized by the feeling that I would be confronted with something unpleasant, as had happened in previous cases. Tense, but calm, I waited a moment. But nothing happened. Innerly triumphant, I then wanted to leave the room. There, before the door, stood a huge person with a hood over his head who immediately lunged at me causing [me] great fear.[75]

In chapter 2, we saw the example of a dreamer whose disapproving mother appeared when he performed wrong or inappropriate activities within his lucid dreams. Seemingly, these activities subconsciously prompted an inner conflict of beliefs, leading to a feeling of guilt, and this emotional energy was transformed into an appropriate symbol—his disapproving mother. Similarly, Tholey consciously noticed how his subconscious expectations of punishment likely led to the creation of a dream figure equal to the task of punishing.

I consider these dream figures to be examples of "thought forms" or dream figures created by the conscious or unconscious mental energy of the lucid dreamer and his or her larger awareness. Thought forms show dream figures at their most basic level (and this probably explains why the disapproving mother could not respond to the dreamer's queries). Put another way, thought forms often represent the expressed reflection of new mental energy in the dream theater at its most basic level.

I recall an example of this from my teenage years. I became lucidly aware when my father criticized me in front of a friend. Now realizing that I was dreaming, I gave my dad a tongue-lashing for embarrassing me. Suddenly, without any conscious intent on my part, a policeman appeared who took my father away.

In this case, the policeman appeared as an unconscious thought form (much like the disapproving mom), unbidden consciously by me but activated by my thoughts and emotions. His sudden appearance at the conclusion of my emotional volley provides a clue to his origin in mental and emotional energy and its associational valence.

On some level, you can think of a thought form within a dream as a figurative representation that expresses a specific feeling or idea.

However, over time, if you have more dreams or life experience associated with that specific feeling or idea, you may add mental and emotional energy to the thought form and possibly help it evolve with more depth and detail. When something like the same conflict is dreamed or experienced repeatedly, it seems plausible that the energy reflected onto the thought form can increase, which leads to its relative permanence and energized nature within the inner platform of dreaming.

As a thought form becomes more energized and fleshed out with greater detail, depth, and vigor, at some point it may achieve a type of consciousness of self within its system (much like a small cutting from a shrub is replanted and becomes aware of itself as a separate plant with new opportunities for growth, even though it once existed as a dependent part of the shrub). In this petri dish of the psyche, a thought form develops or not according to the mental and emotional energy expressed toward it or the issue it represents. With enough repeated additions of energy, it can rise to the level of an independent agent within the dream realm.

Playing with this idea in my own lucid dreams, I sometimes announce: "Now all thought forms must disappear!" In these cases, I intend for all of my dream-figure projections to disappear. Normally, most of them do. However, on occasion, some dream figures remain and look at me with a sense of disbelief that I did not recognize their independence from my thought processes.

Occasionally, lucid dreamers report recurring dream figures, which normally appear to give advice, information, and sometimes commentary on how to manipulate within dreaming. They often serve an educational function. On occasion, lucid dreamers report dream figures who call themselves guides or guardians. Some report meeting deceased loved ones and having conversations much like those that might take place in physical-world meetings. (See chapter 17 in my book, *Lucid Dreaming: Gateway to the Inner Self*.)

Although many may conclude that a deceased dream figure simply represents a projected symbol, memory, or feeling, they can test that assumption when lucidly aware. Some lucid dreamers—like Dutch scientist Frederik van Eeden, who many feel coined the term *lucid dreaming* in 1913—have reported that deceased dream figures provided information that later apparently proved valid. In van Eeden's case, his deceased brother-in-law appeared in a lucid dream and warned him of a future financial loss, which van Eeden felt happened to him.[76]

Through lucid dreaming, you can begin to see that dream figures vary in apparent knowledge, awareness, and capacity to act. Some may seem to be very simple fragments or thought forms within the larger scheme of awareness (which may explain why some can not do any creative or mathematical tasks). Others seem to be more mature independent agents or something akin to sub-personalities. Still others may ask you to consider the possibility of dream visitations. Collectively, they provide a glimpse into the complexity, and even the mystery, of dreaming.

As a lucid dreamer, begin to note the complexity and varied nature of your dream figures. Whether you see it in their alert behavior, thoughtful eyes, or insightful comments, realize that these figures deserve your kindness and respect. And always remember that projecting love, compassion, and understanding onto upset dream figures can transform the situation.

Lucid dreaming has much to teach and, if explored seriously with diverse experiments, can illuminate a new view of the workings of the unconscious.

How to Talk to Dream Figures

When lucid, look for an alert dream figure. If appropriate to the situation, consider the following interactions:

- Politely ask: "What do you represent?" If the response makes sense, consider an appropriate reply (or one conducive to growth, healing, or creativity). If the response does not make sense, try another dream figure who acts or looks more aware.

- Pick up or point out an object in the dream. Ask the figure: "What does this represent?" Does the response seem plausible?

- Point to an object and ask the figure to tell you what it sees. Do you see the same thing it sees?

- Ask the figure to give you a word that rhymes with any word that comes to mind in that moment. If the figure seems talented, ask it to recite a poem or rhyming verse.

- Ask the figure to do a simple multiplication problem. Does it matter whether you mentally conceive of the answer first?

- If you meet a particularly alert dream figure, or one that you have seen before, ask it: "Can you remind me to become lucidly aware the next time we meet in a dream?" Listen to its response.

- If you find yourself in a crowd of dream figures, announce: "Now all my thought forms must disappear!" See what happens.

Chapter 8

INTENT AND THE POWER OF SURRENDER

Numerous scientific studies of non-lucid dreams provide evidence that sleeping and dreaming naturally enhance creativity. Consider these two fascinating examples.

- In the *Proceedings of the National Academy of Sciences*, a research team led by Sara Mednick at the University of California in San Diego offered an associative word test to seventy-seven participants that required a creative solution. Those participants allowed REM sleep showed a 40-percent increase in successfully solving the word test when compared to a control group allowed quiet rest and non-REM sleep. The study suggests that the positive results occur because "REM enhances the formation of associative networks and the integration of unassociated information for creative problem solving."[77]

- In a 2004 study published by the journal *Nature*, researchers at the University of Lübeck in Germany asked participants to solve a difficult math problem. Eight hours later, participants came back to solve a similar math problem, which the researchers knew had a simpler, more elegant solution. Sixty percent of those who had slept during the eight-hour break used this simpler way to solve the problem compared to only 20 percent of non-sleep participants.[78]

Besides scientific research showing that sleep and dreams enhance the likelihood of creative problem-solving, our collective folk wisdom supports this conclusion with the oft-heard advice: "Let's sleep on it and look at it in the morning." Yet in lucid dreaming, you do not need to wait and hope for creativity to occur. You can consciously probe this naturally creative state and experience it directly, particularly when using the power of intent.

Intent offers lucid dreamers immediate access to the incredible creativity and inventiveness of lucid dreams. You can go beyond your waking mind's limitations and touch your inner creativity, your unconscious, perhaps even your muse. This simple lucid dream from March 1983 taught me a lot about how to use the power of intent:

> I found myself in a classroom when it hit me that I had already graduated from college, so I must be dreaming. Feeling lighthearted, I looked around the room and made an announcement. I told the class that I planned to go out in the hall, but when I returned, I wanted to see many more attractive women in here!
>
> I stepped outside with a big grin. Shutting the door behind me, I then thought: "How long do I have to wait here for the attractive women to appear?" After about thirty seconds, I opened the door. There stood a U-shaped line of about fifteen attractive women, all completely unique (blondes, brunettes, redheads, petite, tall, and so on). Not only that, but they stood completely and unashamedly naked. This final detail I did not specifically intend, but found pleasantly surprising and agreeable.

Okay, the intent of this lucid dream seems a bit salacious; after all, I was in my twenties. But consider what happened here. I announced my intent, stepped out of the scene, and then waited for my intent to materialize. In less than thirty seconds, I encountered an extraordinary and detailed scene, created by . . . me? I don't recall creating it. I did not even think: "Well, we need five blondes of various heights, three redheads, some petite brunettes, and a few women with black hair. Oh, and they have to have . . . ." I merely announced my intent.

So who or what answers a lucid dreamer's intent? At first, the answer may seem obvious: Your subconscious or unconscious answers your intent. If correct, this suggests several things:

- The subconscious or unconscious part of you exists with enough awareness to receive your requested intent.

- The subconscious or unconscious part of you has the ability to process your intent's meaning.

- The subconscious or unconscious part of you almost instantly creates the intended forms with incredible detail.

- When you return to the dream setting, the subconscious or unconscious part of you has your intended outcome attractively displayed for your close and personal inspection.

If the unconscious answers a dreamer's proclaimed intent, lucid dreamers apparently encounter a responsive, creative, and purposeful layer of the self. Moreover, when it responds to intent in a lucid dream, the unconscious also provides scientific evidence for another aware layer of the self and expresses a bit about its relationship with you.

On online lucid dreaming forums, there are many examples of lucid dreamers using intent. Rebecca Turner, creator of the online forum *World-of-Lucid-Dreaming.com*, tells of reading my first book and deciding to play with the awareness behind the dream.

In my lucid dream I shouted: *show me something hilarious!* The next thing I saw was a man-sized, multi-colored furry ape walking down the street towards me. He had a groovy walk and his fur ruffled in high-definition. This bizarre, out-of-the-blue image *was* hilarious and I fell into fits of giggles. I was also bemused by my dreaming self's sense of humor.

As you can see, the thoughtful use of intent introduces the magic of lucid dreaming.

Open or Unlimited Intent

The real magic of intent occurs when you modify this process and explore open or unlimited intent. In limited intent, you specify what you wish to see or experience, but in unlimited intent, you make an open-ended request to seek out information unknown to you or creativity beyond your conscious mind. In unlimited intent, you do not specify the exact nature of the experience; rather, you make a request about something whose answer lies outside of your conscious knowledge. In effect, unlimited intent sometimes takes the lucid dreaming you beyond your waking knowing.

By actively playing with intent in lucid dreams, you can explore the depth of lucid dreaming and the depth of the mind. My first example here showed making a request of limited intent. By that, I mean I announced to the dream what I wished or intended ("I want to see many more attractive women in here"). I placed defined limits on the intent and basically specified the general item or action that I wished to see. Then I awaited the response.

Here's another example of limited intent:

> When I saw Paul, he had red hair. But I know he has no hair on his head. I realized: "This is a dream!"
>
> Lucid, I looked around. I saw a building that looked like a garage and decided to intend to find a red Ferrari there. I announced: "When I go into the building, I will find a red Ferrari." I entered the building and found a very nice red Ferrari. I jumped into the driver's seat. The leather felt perfect, and all the instruments looked so detailed. I turned the ignition key and felt the engine roar to life.

In this example, the lucid dreamer defines or specifies the intended object or event (a red Ferrari).

Now consider an example of unlimited intent, provided to me by a young woman. In response to her claim that lucid dreams have no meaning, I suggested that she open up to the creativity of lucid dreaming through unlimited intent. I have edited her dream for brevity.

A lion is chasing me. I hide behind a rock. The lion jumps over the rock to get me, and then I think: "Lions do not run free in Kansas City! This is a lucid dream!" Now I stand up and tell the lion to freeze. I then recall Robert's suggestion and tell the dream: "Show me something important for me to see!"

Suddenly, a long blue hallway appears. I see a woman with white hair near the end of it and go to investigate. It is my great-grandmother. She died almost fifteen years ago, when I was small! We talk. At the end, she says: "Tell your mother to remember the back room in my house." I say: "What?" She repeats: "Tell your mother to remember the back room in my house." I wake.

In this example, the lucid dreamer asks a question or makes a request that seeks a creatively open answer. So unlimited intent does not define or specify a response; it leaves the response open.

After the preceding lucid dream, my friend called her mother and told her about the dream involving her great-grandmother, who wants the mother to remember the back room in her house. Suddenly, the mother burst into tears and told her daughter that the happiest moments in her childhood occurred in the back room of her grandmother's house, where all the grandchildren gathered once a week to play and dress up as kings and queens.

By using unlimited intent, in which the response is not limited by the waking self's direction, we discover instances when lucid dreaming appears to take us beyond the waking self's knowledge and the waking self's limited creative perspective. By using unlimited intent, you can open up to information from the responsive awareness of the unconscious. Or, perhaps, you could call this layer of awareness the inner self. Upon waking, you can normally see the profound creativity behind its response and sometimes even validate the response.

Surrendering Control

In Stephen LaBerge's first book, *Lucid Dreaming*, he states:

[P]ossible pitfalls [exist] on the path of inner growth through lucid dreaming. Primary among them is the tendency for the less than fully lucid dream ego to misunderstand and misuse the new access to power and control over dreams that lucidity brings.[79]

This, he feels, may lead to "ego inflation," and ego-led lucid dream manipulations that fail to acknowledge the interests of the larger self.

Recognizing this as a distinct possibility, LaBerge suggests that lucid dreamers consider "surrendering control from who you *think* you are to who you truly are." To do this, he suggests various approaches to surrender, in which the dreamer lets go of manipulating the lucid dream. Consider doing the following in a lucid dream:

- If religiously inclined, announce in the lucid dream your "submission to the will of God."[80]

- If that seems too spiritual, announce in the lucid dream: "I surrender to the Highest."

- If that all sounds too much, simply announce that you surrender any directing activity.

LaBerge reports that he had "one of the most satisfying experiences of my life" when he surrendered to "the Highest" in a lucid dream.[81] Suddenly, he found himself flying through space, past religious symbols, to a "vast mystical realm" filled with love, whereupon he spontaneously began to sing a song of praise. Other experienced lucid dreamers have also felt surprised by the extraordinary occurrences they have experienced when they simply decided to surrender in their lucid dreams.

In the online magazine *Lucid Dreaming Experience*, I interviewed a talented lucid dreamer and therapist, Mary Ziemer, who uses lucid dreaming for many purposes, including spiritual growth.[82] As such, she frequently surrenders in her lucid dreams and sees where the experience takes her. Following is a short list of guidelines for surrendering in a lucid dream, based on articles by Ziemer.

- Let go of any conscious expectations, intent, or sense of controlling the outcome.

- Recognize your fundamental sense of trust and allowance.

- Acknowledge any sense of fear that you may feel and move through it.

- Express your intent to surrender.

- Allow unusual experiences to take place. You may find yourself moving through imageless space, or you may let go of your dream body and become a point of perception; allow the experience.

- If you feel a spontaneous response inside of you, express it naturally. Feel a sense of trust.

Of course, the idea of surrender brings up the issue of to whom or what the lucid dreamer surrenders. LaBerge initially remains silent on identifying who or what responds to his intent to surrender, writing: "Such questions as whether this is a part of yourself or something beyond yourself need not be resolved at this point." In a later book, he puts it thus: "To go beyond the ego's model of the world, the lucid dreamer must relinquish control of the dream—surrender—to something beyond the ego."[83]

Almost thirty years have elapsed since LaBerge broached the idea of surrender in lucid dreams. Since that time, some lucid dreamers have come to the point of wanting to resolve "whether this [the response to surrendering] is a part of yourself or something beyond yourself," and what it means when surrender takes you to "something beyond the ego."

These questions of who or what responds when you surrender or practice unlimited intent in a lucid dream have fundamental importance for the field of psychology, because these examples appear to show interactions with a responsive layer of conscious awareness.

Who responds? What responds?

Lucid dreaming has potential to become a revolutionary psychological tool to explore both dreaming and the larger psyche. By using open or unlimited intent, lucid dreamers appear to discover strong evidence for a responsive inner awareness—and perhaps much more.

Carl Jung spent decades investigating the nature of dreams, dream figures, the unconscious, and the psyche. His work continues to have a profound impact on the science of psychology and psychotherapy through his writings and ideas. In a portion of that work, he suggested that the unconscious may contain conscious awareness. If this is so, he argues, this would need to show certain characteristics:

> We have no knowledge of how this unconscious functions, but since it is conjectured to be a psychic system it may possibly have everything that consciousness has, including perception, apperception, memory, imagination, will, affectivity, feeling, reflection, judgment, etc., all in subliminal form.[84]

When lucid dreamers have used intent to pose questions and requests to the invisible awareness in lucid dreams, all of these nine characteristics have appeared in the response. Reports of these lucid dreams appear to provide evidentiary support for Jung's suggestion of another layer of consciousness within the psychic system of the unconscious.

Jung continues this line of thinking:

> If the unconscious can contain everything that is known to be a function of consciousness, then we are faced with the possibility that it too, like consciousness, possesses a subject, a sort of ego . . . [which] brings out the real point of my argument: the fact, namely, that a second psychic system coexisting with consciousness—no matter what qualities we suspect it of possessing—is of absolutely revolutionary significance in that it could radically alter our view of the world.[85]

Because many independently reported lucid dreams use surrender or open-ended intent, they appear to show that this inner awareness possesses all the characteristics of consciousness that Jung lists. As such, lucid dreaming does provide apparent evidence for a second psychic system coexisting with consciousness, which Jung claims to be "of absolutely revolutionary significance in that it could radically alter our view of the world."

LaBerge holds back from identifying who or what responds to his act of surrender. It seems, however, that Jung may have inadvertently supplied the criteria for the issue's resolution, while experienced lucid dreamers have provided the evidence in their self-reports of using surrender and unlimited intent. Lucid dreaming, although somewhat ignored by psychology and physics, may thus become an invaluable tool for scientifically verifying the existence of a second psychic system coexisting with consciousness.

Limited vs. Unlimited Intent

Through using both types of lucid dream intent—limited and unlimited—you learn how they can result in very different and distinct outcomes. When you specify the intent, your inner awareness normally calls forth a very detailed mental model that looks, feels, sounds, and possibly even smells and tastes like the physical-reality version. This inner awareness responds to your limited, specified intent instantly, often adding details that seem emotionally embedded in the intent, though unstated—like attractive women (the stated intent) without any clothing (unstated, but emotionally implied in the specified intent).

Some call limited intent the agent for procuring mental models. Inside your mind, psychology maintains, you hold a vast supply of mental models of nearly every conceivable shape, size, type, and dimension. Imagine a white bear. Now imagine a white bear on a sandy beach drinking a cocktail. Now imagine a white bear on a sandy beach drinking a cocktail in front of a large cruise ship. Your mind can call forth these mental models with stunning alacrity in your imagination when you focus and intend to do so.

However, when lucid dreamers use open or unlimited intent, they open the field to unknown responses, which potentially allows them to go beyond mental models to unexpected experiences that show original creativity, sometimes outside of their knowing. By using unlimited intent, lucid dreamers gain even greater access to naturally abundant creativity (which science shows exists) and inventiveness. In a way, using unlimited intent in lucid dreaming allows a dreamer to move beyond the waking self's knowing to the seemingly broader knowing of an inner awareness.

Lucid dreamers use open or unlimited intent in various fashions and refer to it in various ways, even as "surrender." When you use unlimited intent you may:

- Notice that a lucid dream experience seems largely a co-creation of both your waking self and an inner awareness or inner self.

- Realize that you can pose thoughtful questions in a lucid dream and begin to determine the width and breadth of the inner self's knowledge and responsiveness.

- Ask to experience concepts—"Let me feel unconditional love!" or "Let me experience a simple fear that limits my growth."

- Ask for expressions of creativity—"Show me the most incredible piece of art that I can paint at this time!" or "Let me hear the lyrics to a beautiful new song that I can write!"

- Seek out information on new inventions and/or resolutions to real-world problems.

- Explore the nature of time and space, or of consciousness and the mind.

A thoughtful person may wonder how you know whether your unlimited intent has actually resulted in original creativity or inventiveness. How do you know it does not result in random responses or incoherent experiences? The normally successful responses to lucid dreamers' limited or specified intent give a general indication that this level of awareness seeks to comply with your specific request. In cases of unlimited intent, lucid dreamers and outside observers can often see how the intent engenders a truly creative and inventive response (which does not appear random or incoherent).

How to Use Limited and Unlimited Intent

Think about what you may want to explore. Write out six simple requests, but make three of them of limited intent (e.g., "Let me see a red Ferrari when I open the door") and three of unlimited intent that allow for an open-ended response (e.g., "Show me something important for me to see."). Use only requests that you believe possible to experience.

A third situation exists, however, that offers additional support for the creative intelligence behind the response. It involves cases in which the larger awareness rebuffs the lucid dreamer's specified intent. Here's an example:

> An experienced lucid dreamer, PasQuale, agrees to conduct an experiment with participants in her popular lucid dreaming forum, *www.LD4all.com*. The group makes this lofty goal: Once lucid, find the beginning and end of the universe. PasQuale becomes lucid, recalls the task, and asks: "Show me the beginning and end of the Universe!" She hears a voice respond: "The Universe has no beginning or end. The Universe is an everlasting cycle."[86]

Here, you see a simple example of this inner awareness refuting the lucid dreamer's request, qualifying its reasoning for doing so and offering a creative answer.

In this chapter, we have seen that a specified or limited intent will normally provide what you request—a red Ferrari or a unicorn. However, when you open up the field of possibilities and use unlimited intent, your larger awareness normally responds in an educational, instructive, and creative manner. By using unlimited intent, you can develop a knowledgeable relationship with your larger awareness and get some sense of the true depth of your psyche.

Chapter 9

RESPONDING EFFECTIVELY
IN YOUR DREAMS

The famous scientist Louis Pasteur said: "Chance favors the prepared mind." By reading and rereading this book, you prepare your mind to take advantage of lucid dreaming at the moment it happens. Moreover, by completing the practices in this book, you actually think of how to respond to many lucid dream situations.

Most people need little instruction in how to respond to creative, constructive, and fulfilling lucid dreams. Embracing the energy, warmth, and positive emotions in these types of dreams seems quite natural for most of us. If anything, we wake with a sense of wonder and a hope to go even deeper into the beauty of our inner realms.

However, when you encounter perplexing, emotional, or recurring lucid dream situations, it helps to have some strategies in mind. This is even more true on those rare occasions when you find yourself encountering something alarming. In these cases, it helps to have ideas of how best to respond.

Making Thoughtful Responses

Let's look at some examples of experienced lucid dreamers and how they responded to difficult dreams. In an interview with PasQuale Ourtane,[87] she tells of how she responded to a potentially frightful situation:

> Once, I had a dream in which a German soldier from WWII was coming after me to make me prisoner or something. I

ran down a bridge and hid myself in a corner. Then I realized I was dreaming.

"I want to know who that is chasing after me and why he's doing it," I said to myself. I yelled: "Here I am! Come and catch me!" There he came. But the mean-looking soldier had transformed into a small childlike woman.

I asked: "Who are you?"

She replied: "I'm your fear for the unknown."

This was a very emotional moment in the dream and, crying, I hugged her.

I realized that my "fear for the unknown" had made me "run away" in real-life situations.

Once lucid, PasQuale realized that she had little to fear and much to gain by understanding what chased her. Notice how she responds by calling the dream figure to come closer and removing the sense of separation. Also, notice how she questions the figure to help determine its meaning. Finally, notice how she responds in a heartfelt manner to the realization by hugging the figure. From PasQuale's actions, you can take away these general lessons or principles:

- Seek information and understanding when pursued.

- Face the figure or situation and question it in an open-ended manner.

- Respond to the new information from the heart.

In this situation, a lucid dreamer could have done virtually anything—flown away, fought with the figure, stopped the dream, and so on—but you need to realize that each response has ramifications. If you fly away, what do you gain? If you fight, what do you learn? If you stop the entire dream, what happens to the interactive relating?

When you look at common nightmare dream reports, what happens? Dreamers normally respond in one of two ways: fight or flight. They run from the monster or try to fight it. But for a lucid dreamer, fight or flight seems a false dichotomy or a false set of only two possible choices. Lucid dreaming opens up new possibilities in which dreamers hopefully see that many more options and responses exist. In fact, the solution to many dreaming and waking nightmares comes in seeking out and expressing new creative responses. Many possibilities exist between the extremes of fight or flight if you open up to them.

Paul Tholey reports an interesting lucid dream[88] that illustrates the importance of thoughtful response. While being chased by a tiger, he becomes lucid and asks it: "Who are you?" The tiger suddenly transforms into his father and announces: "I am your father and will now tell you what you are to do!" Tholey considers how to respond and decides not to "beat him" or attack him, but to try to dialogue with him.

In the ensuing conversation, Tholey states that his father cannot order him around. He turns away from his insults and threats, but then realizes that some of his father's criticism seems justified and decides to change his behavior. With this change of heart, suddenly his father becomes friendly. They shake hands. Tholey asks his father to help him, but his father urges him to find his own way. At the conclusion, Tholey notes that the image of his father slips into his body, and he remains alone in the dream.

Apparently, Tholey had tried to attack or "beat him" in other dreams, but in this one realized that a dialogue offered more chances for resolution. He writes that he rejects "his threats and insults" while listening to some of the criticisms, which seem "justified." Then Tholey makes the inner decision to change his behavior, based on what he has learned. Interestingly, at the exact moment of Tholey's inner change, his father becomes friendly and they shake hands. Now Tholey basically accepts the figure of the father, who then slips "into my own body."

As a lesson in lucid dreaming, Tholey's dream behavior here offers these guidelines:

- Respond thoughtfully to lucid dream situations and consider the alternatives to aggressive situations beyond simple fight or flight.

- Question aggressive figures in an open-ended manner.

- Listen and accept valid points; agree to change when warranted.

- Ask for the dream figure's help; if possible, accept the dream figure.

In this next example, you see an experienced lucid dreamer, who faces a similar situation, but chooses a different approach in responding:

> I am in the living room of one of my childhood homes. I hear my father yelling very loudly. He sounds very angry and I am afraid. I try to find him, but I don't know where he is. Now I see him. He is coming down the hallway into the living room. He looks to be about eight feet tall. He looks angry. I realize that this is a dream and I remember that I should try to show him love rather than run away or fight. I walk up to him and hug him. He turns into my childhood dog, whom I loved very much.[89]

The above example (used by persmission) from the book, *A Dream Come True*, by author and lucid dreamer, David L. Kahn in Minneapolis, provides a new response: showing love, compassion, acceptance, and understanding to fearful figures or negative energy.[3] When lucid dreamers respond by projecting compassion, the angry or fearful figure or object often dissolves and becomes transformed.

While writing this chapter, another lucid dreamer, Jennifer, sent me an interesting lucid dream (below) that shows a more complex response to difficult dream figures. Jennifer then asks some important questions. First the lucid dream, then the questions:

> Last night, I dreamed I was with two men and then I suddenly saw a narrow lighted sort of alley but realized it was a passageway. I immediately wanted to find out about it and go through it. When I walked towards it, I suddenly realized that I must be dreaming. So I turned to the two men and told them: "I'm dreaming!"
>
> Suddenly, this other guy rushed towards me and held both my arms tightly while I pushed back against the

force. I wasn't too afraid or fearful, and I remembered to give him thoughts of love or be centered enough to give him thoughts of love, but my concentration seems divided between trying to give him thoughts of love and resisting the force of him holding my arms and also I felt he was squishing my chest. . . .

I was waiting for the man to dissolve or disappear as I gave him thoughts of love. I struggled to be centered, but somehow the effort was difficult as my attention was divided between resisting his force and meditating [on thoughts of love]. I wasn't afraid of him or what was happening, though. And then the dream changed to me attending a class.

Jennifer asked: "Is this my fear showing up? Or is this energy from outside of myself? How can I know the difference?" It seems appropriate that the dream ends with Jennifer "attending a class," because this experience looks like a valuable lesson in lucid dreaming. Looking at her dream, can you name other creative responses that Jennifer could have made to this situation? Does her focus in the lucid dream seem unified or divided?

In this situation, Jennifer later realized that she could have asked the dream figure questions to gain understanding: "What do you represent?" or "Who are you?" By understanding what you face, you often have an easier time resolving it successfully in the dream state.

In addition, she noted that dividing her energy between resisting and trying to send thoughts of love took her in two different directions. Like stepping on the brake and pushing on the gas at the same time, these entirely different responses will probably result in little real change or resolution. Having a unified focus seems much better when creating a response. Finally, remember that a sense of listening to any advice from your inner intuition seems important, because you may get creative solutions on how to respond.

Please realize that projecting love and compassion in a lucid dream requires a true and focused sense of empathy. The dream or dream figure will respond to the exact flavor, intensity, and depth of the projected compassion. A small bit of compassion projected outward will elicit a small response. Compassion mixed with anxiety will show a different response. Real depth of feeling for the suffering of the other will strengthen the connection and accelerate the response. None of us can fake it in the dynamic state of dreaming. And in responding to difficult dreams, every lucid dreamer will face his or her own unique issues.

When you show real compassion, acceptance, and understanding, it appears to elicit a response in equal measure to the depth, purity, and intensity that you offer. A response that comes sincerely from the heart can transform virtually every situation. And when lucid dreamers respond by projecting compassion, angry or fearful dream figures or objects often dissolve or become transformed. In the lucid dreams of PasQuale and Tholey, you can see how the simple desire to understand who was chasing them resulted in the frightful figure of a Nazi soldier turning into a childlike woman and a tiger turning into the father. It seems that the simple desire to understand transmutes fearful energy into something more benign. This seems more pronounced in the case of Kahn, who lucidly projects love onto the fearful figure, then sees it transformed into his childhood dog.

After years as a lucid dreamer, I made it a general policy to go to the area of the most-sensed energy or emotion (positive or negative) in my dreams. I did this because I could see that lucid dreaming naturally led to healing, education, and resolving inner struggles. The broader perspective of lucid dreams resulted in more understanding, from which emerged more thoughtful and compassionate responses. Through lucid dreaming, I could see an organic path to greater integration and harmony, and not an external system of rules and responses applied to all situations.

How to Make Thoughtful Responses

Make it a habit to examine your responses thoughtfully within a lucid dream. The following questions may help:

• Do my responses seem instinctive or reactive?

• Do my responses seem habitual?

- Do my responses seem fear-based?

- Do my responses seem constructive?

- Do my responses lead to successful resolutions?

Avoiding Habitual Responses

In lucid dreaming, as in life, you can ignore your amazing creative potential and simply fall into routine patterns or habits. Habitual responses can have many facets: habitual behaviors (e.g., lucid dream sex), habitual emotions (e.g., a need to defend), habitual thinking (e.g., nothing matters but my needs), and so on.

Although being erotically entwined in your lucid dreams can seem very enticing at first, a recurring fixation on this may ultimately bore you, because it hampers your natural growth and development as a lucid dreamer. When you get to the point that it bores you, move on to explore the depths of lucid dreaming. Or, better yet, investigate what lies behind your habitual behavior and understand your actions more clearly.

Occasionally, these habits or habitual ways of thinking may be a type of defense mechanism based on a fear or concern, as seen in this lucid dream[90] from *The Lucid Dream Exchange* (used by permission of the dreamer, who prefers to remain anonymous):

> A Dreamer, July 9, 2011, "Flying and Seeking"
> [Lucid] I come down in an area of lawns and trees, like a college campus. The day seems to be sunny. I want to create wind. I do so and feel the gentle breeze on my face and see the swaying branches and leaves. Next I get the idea to seek "God" or "the highest" but am skeptical of anything convincing happening. I lift off, fly a little, breaking through walls as I lose the visuals. I feel a bit uneasy. Nothing much happens. I think perhaps I am afraid of being overwhelmed.
> Then I am in a room with a woman who tells me I should read a book by a certain author. I have heard of

the author, but not that particular book. She tells me I am afraid of what will happen if I experience the Divine, afraid of how it will change my life. She hands me the cover of the book she recommended.

Notice how the lucid dreamer has a conflicting set of mental reactions—on the one hand, surrendering or seeking God or the highest; on the other hand, feeling skeptical about what may happen. This inner conflict leads to "nothing much" and a slight sense of fear of being overwhelmed. Then an apparently aware dream figure offers an overview and "tells me I am afraid of what will happen if I experience the Divine, afraid of how it will change my life."

Here you see how a lucid dreamer can engage in a habit of skeptical thinking, which disempowers a possible growth experience by putting self-conceived limits on it. Unlike responding with a truly open process, this dreamer feels threatened by the implications of seeking "the highest" and thwarts a real investigation.

Situations like this illustrate the vast distance between acceptance and rejection. A complete acceptance of an issue in a lucid dream allows for its full consideration, response, and resolution. But when you completely reject an issue, figure, or question, no resolution occurs, yet the mental energy remains—and most likely adds energy to a shadow creation that will return. Of course, all the in-between levels of acceptance or rejection are expressed appropriately in the inner-energy equation.

The primary issue, however, involves looking at your habits of behavior, emotion, and thinking. If you notice in lucid dreams that you have a habit of flying away from all conflicts, ask yourself why. If you notice in lucid dreams that you avoid any type of letting go or surrender, investigate the reasons. See whether these habits exist in your waking life as well. Discover your own inner belief system.

How to Identify Habitual Responses

On a sheet of paper, write out a dream or lucid dream that featured an action that required a response.

- List three habitual responses you routinely make.

- Write down three brilliant responses that you could have made.

- List three middle-way responses that fall somewhere between routine and brilliant.

See how a practice like this expands what seems possible and increases your mental flexibility. By having to consider alternatives, you expand the contours of your habitual mind and expectations.

―――

Listen to Your Heart

Ideally, lucid dreaming should encourage a flexible nature, along with an ability to listen to the heart or your intuitions. In some lucid dreams, you will sense or feel intuitional prompts to respond in new ways and, perhaps, with more openness, creativity, or compassion. Experienced lucid dreamers learn to trust these inner prompts and insights, and to see them as a type of guidance in the basic infinity of possible responses.

The following lucid dream, taken from a presentation by Dr. Scott Sparrow, exemplifies the power of thoughtful response.[91] Like a modern parable, it shows layers of self-resistance being overcome in one lucid dream and the transformative power of that new trust, acceptance, and fearlessness.

I am in a cabin alone, and the door opens. Three figures enter and stand abreast just inside the doorway: Dracula, Werewolf, and Frankenstein. I am alarmed, but the strangeness of this event convinces me that I must be dreaming. Realizing that they are only a dream, and that I can make them go away, I say, "You are only a dream. Go away!" They disappear immediately.

Alone again, I think to myself, "Maybe I should have surrounded myself with light instead." So I call out to them to return. The door opens again, and they come back in. I say to myself, "I surround myself with light." Instantly, a pinkish white glow envelops me. As for the figures, I can barely see them through the bright haze.

Then I think, "Maybe I should invite them into the light." So I say, "Please come into the light." As they walk forward, the light fills me, and I experience an overwhelming sense of ecstatic love. Following the dream, I remained in a blissful state for several days.

Here, the lucid dreamer initially responds by rejecting the monsters and acting from a sense of fear. Then he reconsiders and uses a type of protection before opening the door again, although this protective action makes it difficult to see clearly (an interesting and telling detail). Finally, he moves away from rejection and fear and toward acceptance. Inviting the monsters into the light suddenly fills him with light and an overwhelming sense of ecstatic love.

In this example, the dynamic nature of lucid dreaming becomes apparent as the dreamer rethinks and modifies the response three times in relation to the experience, thus reaping the new energy of the responses. The most energy comes when the final response allows even more completion, resolution, and integration. Lucid dreaming allows for this kind of presence in the moment, of which Eckhart Tolle wrote: "Inner alignment with the present moment opens your consciousness and brings it into alignment with the whole, of which the present moment is an integral part. The whole, the totality of life, then acts through you."[92]

Sometimes, a dream figure leads the way, and then the dreamer must decide how to respond, as in this lucid dream[93] by Kelly:

I don't remember all the details except the part where I became aware that I was dreaming. I saw my mother (who passed away ten years ago) sitting in a chair smiling at me. I became aware I was dreaming because in my dream I knew she had passed.

I began to cry in my dream. My mother began crying also. It was like saying goodbye to her again. I began sobbing harder as I looked at my mom. Then all of a sudden, she started making funny faces. Ones that used to make me laugh when she was alive. I began laughing and so did she. There was a sense of peace that came over me. I then woke up. I don't believe I controlled this dream, unless it was subconsciously, but it was an amazing experience.

Here, the dream figure apparently recognizes the lucidity of the dreamer, because she begins to make funny faces as she did when she was alive. These elicit laughter and a sense of peace in the dreamer, who initially felt utter grief. You may wonder whether the dream figure of the mother appeared by virtue of an inner need of Kelley's, or came as a dream visitation by the deceased to help her daughter overcome her grief.

Don't Get Lost in the Big Picture

Sometimes, lucid dreamers carry in their projected mental overlay of beliefs, expectations, and feelings a big-picture idea of the ultimate goal of lucid dreaming. For some spiritual devotees, this may mean enlightenment. For another on the path, it may mean complete freedom or wholeness. Even more big-picture ideas of the ultimate goal of lucid dreaming emerge as you look at the field of psychology, shamanism, and other paths.

Having a broad, flexible goal seems generally fine. However, goalbound lucid dreamers must avoid becoming insensitive and blind to important issues as they seek their ego-selected goals (however grand they seem). What if, in the process of using lucid dreaming to seek enlightenment, important issues about anger arise? For example, dreamers notice that each time they become lucid, they see angry confrontations or angry dream figures.

Because of their deep devotion to their goal of enlightenment, these lucid dreamers may repeatedly ignore these scenes of anger because they are not in keeping with their goals. Instead, they focus on the lucid dreams of light, harmony, and truth. Yet the angry imagery persists and becomes more energetic, even intrusively active. Now they have to respond. At this point, the energy of these angry dream figures may convince them of one of three things:

- The angry dream figures seek to block their progress toward the true goal.

- They must do battle with these figures and their dark anger.

- Even more troubling, they literally have to struggle with dark forces.

These types of dreams illustrate how goal-focused lucid dreamers can ignore legitimate personal issues as they strive toward the ultimate goal, until these ignored issues become huge shadow figures with independent agency. Unfortunately, when the issues become that big and powerful, these dreamers can hardly accept them as personal reflections and often seek some other external explanation. As you read this book and do these practices, realize that you must take the time to clear out intrapersonal issues and limiting beliefs if you plan to use lucid dreaming for deep transformative goals. By focusing on the area of the most energy in your lucid dreams, you will normally arrive at the issues that you need to resolve in order to make progress.

Ancient Greek and Roman myths tell the stories of gods and semi-divine personages who had amazing powers and gifts, but often ignored their weaknesses or misused their powers. These cautionary tales serve as real lessons in lucidity. However, when you use lucid dreaming as a means to know your larger self and faithfully work through issues and limiting beliefs, you open up the path for clearer, more insightful exploration. Goals, frameworks, and ideals have definite value, but if you use them to ignore important situations appearing in your lucid dreams, then they work against you.

Chapter 10

EXPLORING INNER SPACE

Historical accounts suggest that the first telephone call occurred as a result of two fortunate accidents that happened to Alexander Graham Bell. The first and less-known very valuable blunder occurred when Bell read a paper in German, "On the Sensations of Tone," by physicist Hermann von Helmholtz. In it, Bell misinterpreted some German words and came to believe that the publication stated that vowel sounds could be transmitted over a wire. Later, Bell remarked on the value of this blunder: "It gave me confidence. If I had been able to read German, I might never have begun my experiments in electricity."[94]

The more famous accident reportedly happened in Bell's laboratory on March 10, 1876. There, Bell spilled some liquid battery acid and announced: "Mr. Watson, come here. I want you!" In a nearby room, Watson heard Bell's voice come through the phone wire, and he responded to the world's first phone call.

Of equal interest in the history of communication is the work of Italian Guglielmo Marconi, who created a functional wireless telegraphy or radio in 1895, allowing sound to move long distances without connective wires. When Marconi wrote to the Italian Ministry of Post and Telegraphs asking for funding for this radical new device, it seems the minister wrote "to the Longara" (a nearby insane asylum in Rome) about the request. Marconi sought assistance from more supportive countries and moved to London in 1896. By 1897, he had numerous requests to demonstrate his remarkable device around the world.

Now fast-forward eighty years and consider someone claiming that a sleeping person can consciously communicate by eye signals when lucid dreaming. Consider the mechanics of the lucid-communication process: The conscious dreaming mind induces the physical brain to signal the mind's awareness by moving the dreaming eyes left to right in the dream scene, which causes the physical eyes to move and the REM polygraph machine to record the movement as scientific evidence. In these eye-signal-verified lucid dreams, the dreamer communicates both to the physical body and to the outside world.[95]

However, lucid dreaming also shows us that lucid dreamers communicate with the inner realm of dream figures, objects, and settings—and, apparently, with another layer of awareness, as seen in the use of surrender and intent. Here, lucid dreamers can often discover what dream figures represent, work through personal issues, practice physical skills, seek creativity, and more. Lucid dreaming thus allows us to see that the dream state can function as a platform for multi-level communicating, accessing information and using mental energy. Like Marconi's breakthrough, lucid dreaming demonstrates the functional reality of a revolutionary new tool for communicating inner explorations to outer realms. It opens a vast new field for scientific exploration and experimentation in dreaming, the unconscious, and the larger psyche.

In this chapter, we look at the practice and pitfalls of experimenting within lucid dreams—or perhaps you could say experimenting within the laboratory of the mind. In these situations, lucid dreamers need to consider various items that influence the experimental results and how to manage an experiment, even when it goes awry.

A Dreamtime Search Engine

Consciously aware in a lucid dream, you can seek virtually any information and experiment with virtually any topic, even things outside of your own experience, imagination, or mental models. Of course, limits seem to exist—some of them within you and your belief system. So in this mental laboratory, it helps to have a sense of how other lucid dreamers have managed to investigate, explore, and communicate with the contents of their unconscious mind successfully.

In May 1985, Ed Kellogg had a lucid dream that gave him insight into a technique to gather clear information—something he later called a "dreamtime search engine to successfully access information of all kinds." He formalized these insights into the Lucid Dream

Information Technique (LDIT) and wrote about it in an article in the *Dream Network Bulletin*.[96] In this update,[97] he recalls the initial lucid dream inspiration, then gives his explanation of the technique:

In a lucid dream, I demonstrate an incubation technique using a silver bowl to a group of other [dreamers]. Basically, the technique consisted of the following. First the lucid dreamer decides on a question, in which he or she asks for the information most needed at that time. After deciding on a specific question, the dreamer inverts the silver bowl and consciously focuses on the question. After waiting a few seconds for the answer to materialize, the dreamer then turns over the bowl to find a materialized note with the answer written on it. I took a number of my fellow [dreamers] through this incubation technique, and each received a clear and discrete answer. For myself I asked for a message from an official in a government agency about the possibilities of future research grants and received the answer "Good bye!" which I clearly understood meant that I would receive no further funding from this agency (note: which incidentally, proved quite true).

Since that time, I've experimented with variations of the LDIT, which one can break down into four steps: (1) finding a medium for the materialization of the answer (such as a closed drawer or blank piece of paper); (2) asking the question, waiting a few seconds (important!); (3) opening the drawer (or turning over the paper, etc.) and seeing what has materialized; and, finally, (4) memorizing what you see, waking yourself up from LDR (Lucid Dream Reality) and then accurately and completely recording the information in WPR (Waking Physical Reality).

If I open a drawer, sometimes I find a written note or drawing; at other times, an object or objects symbolizing the answer appears. And as for reading, I need to read it clearly the first time through, as rereading messages usually doesn't work very well for me. Some materializing mediums work far better than others, and the best give discrete, specific answers, easily remembered in the transition from LDR to WPR. One can, for example, ask the question and then turn over a piece of dream paper, open a dream book, turn on a dream television, or even type the question into a dream computer and press Enter to display the answer.

Finding a suitable medium may require some ingenuity on your part—not every dreamscape has empty drawers, blank pieces of paper, or silver bowls lying about! In order to use the LDIT, I need to maintain a clear-headed lucidity throughout the incubation process and then consciously retain and clearly recall the answer on returning to WPR.

As an oracle of information, I've found the LDIT very useful and the information received usually of a very high quality. This does not mean that I always get usable answers to the questions I ask! In one case, where I had requested investment information, I received my answer on a clay tablet in what looked like cuneiform! I've used the LDIT as a kind of dreamtime search engine to successfully access information of all kinds, from remote viewing targets to investment advice. However, to begin, I suggest that you first use the LDIT to obtain information on improving health and healing, either for yourself or for someone you care about.

In this technique, the lucid dreamer essentially uses intent to request information along with the location of its appearance. For example, you can request that the desired information or intent will appear in the next room when you open the door, or you can request that it will appear behind you when you turn around. In some cases, when I have tried this, the request materialized in the sky above me or resulted in a complete transformation of the entire visual scene.

Just as when entering key words into an Internet search engine, lucid dreamers have to pay attention to the exact wording for their intent. This explains why some devise the wording of their intent in the waking state). Take the intent: "When I turn around, I will look *for* the answer to my question." In this case, you may spend the entire lucid dream looking *for* the answer. Now take the intent: "When I turn around, I will look *at* the answer to my question." In this case, you will likely turn around and find yourself looking *at* some representation of the answer. So keep in mind that even the minor nuance of a preposition (*for* or *at*) can alter the direction of your intent and result in major changes.

Rationally, you should develop a track record of success with this process before relying on it. If you seek out information and the response seems clear, understandable, and valid in 80 percent of the cases, then you know that you have an 80-percent success ratio. On the other hand, if you find that the requested information appears in cuneiform or in unclear symbols in half the cases, you may need to work on either your process of requesting information (expressing a clear intent) or on your belief system and mental overlay (fear about what you may discover).

In addition, you need to understand that, in the LDIT process and in using unlimited intent, the question or request is normally asked of the invisible larger awareness in the dream (the unconscious mind, if you prefer). Lucid dreamers simply announce it. Some turn their heads up to the sky and request it. The main point here is that you seek the information from your larger awareness, however you wish to define that term.

By contrast, you should use caution in asking these same questions or requests of most dream figures. Lucid dreamers report frequent difficulty with understanding the responses of dream figures. Since the dream figures may represent some smaller aspect of you, they normally have relatively less awareness than you and often provide unclear or incoherent answers. In effect, the success ratio for questions asked of dream figures seems lower than for those asked of the larger awareness. Some exceptions exist—deceased dream figures you know personally, or radiantly aware dream figures—but, on the whole, avoid asking unexceptional dream figures important questions or requesting important information from them.

Managing Experiments

Because lucid dreamers can try virtually any experiment within a lucid dream, it seems vitally important to realize that they report that they can successfully end their experiments by simply announcing commands like "Cancel" or "Stop." If you ever find yourself in a situation that gets too uncomfortable, issue a command to cancel or stop the process.

Occasionally, experienced lucid dreamers find themselves in a curious predicament. They want to learn about a concept and ask to experience it, but as the concept unfolds, a lot of energy, information, and material come along with it. This can feel quite intense. In a lucid dream, I once wondered aloud about the nature of *chi* or *qi* (energy) and then watched an amazing explanation of sorts materialize in front of me. For a brief moment, I had some concern; but then I realized that my larger awareness rarely involved me in something beyond my capacity to experience, so I let go of my concern and patiently watched. At the end, in a moment of joy, I merged with the powerful *chi*, and it felt incredible.

For some people, making broad conceptual requests in a lucid dream—like "Let me experience Divine Grace!"—may result in a conceptual experience of such power and beauty that it feels breathtaking. In such cases, if it seems like too much, you may need to announce a command to change the intensity of the experience. Lucid dreamer Jeffrey Peck agreed to share his lucid dream[98] of asking to experience the concept of Divine Grace.

> I'm in a bank watching some kids eat cookies. This seems strange and I become lucid and walk out of the bank. I walk through the parking lot and see a small school. I yell out my request, but my voice doesn't sound louder than my surroundings. I muster all of my will and emotion and yell out to the dream space above me, "Let me experience Divine Grace!"
>
> I hear a strange noise, and a vortex appears above me. I fall into a void and I feel intense oneness and calmness. I see the solar system and all of space before me. I understand that the Supreme Intelligence, whether you call it God, Tao, Brahman, Atman, Christ, designed the entire universe and everything in it. I feel a powerful presence and voidness. At the same time I can feel myself laying [sic] on a sticky material like concrete. I can grab the concrete underneath my hands like silly putty or Play-Doh.

The experience ends and I'm in a living room. I don't know what to experience next, so I yell out, "Let me experience Bliss!" The noise begins again, and a vortex appears. I get the feeling this will feel very powerful and cancel before anything happens. My vision becomes very distorted and I wake shortly after.

As you can see, Peck decides to seek out a second experience, but intuitively knows this may feel too powerful. So he decides to cancel the request. As a result, the experience stops and he wakes up. Again, your experiences with concepts can result in unexpected transformations and exceptionally intense situations. Lucid dreamers need to realize this, so that, when necessary, they can stop the process by announcing their intent to do so.

A few lucid dreamers have reported instances in which an unseen voice announces that their request needs more consideration. One dreamer reported making a profound request to experience a concept in modern physics. A voice told him that he seemed too unfocused and distracted to try an experiment like this at that time. The voice went on to suggest that he try again when clearer and more mindful.

Some lucid dreamers have sought unique information and then felt perplexed when strange mathematical formulas and geometric shapes came flying through space in response. Some lucid dream experiments may require you to ask for the perceived response to come in a manner that you can fathom.

As you can see, the requested experience often feels completely unexpected, profound, and incredible. You may wonder whether the response seems similar to what others have independently experienced. It does seem possible to check a lucid dreamer's report against the experience of other lucid dreamers using the same protocol and similar intent and wording. And, in some experiments involving waking physical reality, you can check the information received in the lucid dream against information obtainable in the waking world. In this way, lucid dreamers can possibly gather evidence for information coming from some type of collective unconscious.

Just How Lucid Are Lucid Dreams?

This question serves as the title of a research study by Harvard Medical School psychologist Deirdre Barrett.[99] Using fifty lucid dream subjects, Barrett cites a number of lucid dreams in which the dreamers engage in irrational thought. She also examines the dream reports along four corollaries that she feels a truly lucid dreamer should realize:

- People in dreams are dream characters.

- Dream objects are not real—that is, actions will not carry over concretely on awakening.

- Dreamers do not need to obey waking-life physics to achieve a goal.

- Memory of the waking world is intact rather than amnestic or fictitious.

From reading some lucid dreamers' self-reports, you may find yourself agreeing with Dr. Barrett. It does seem silly for lucid dreamers to flap their arms like birds in order to fly in a dream. When looking at your own lucid dreams, you may think upon waking: "Why did I ask the dream figure of my sister to take notes about the lucid dream and then give them to me in the morning? How silly to think a dream figure will have notes for me the next day!"

In the lucid dream state, however, you exist within a dynamic matrix of beliefs or projected mental overlay in each moment. Your actions seem thoughtful, intelligent, and rational *within that specific matrix of beliefs*. So essentially, they do seem rational or lucid. However, when you wake and possess your waking belief system, these same actions may appear errant, silly, or irrational. It helps to understand this point so that you can relate your responses and actions to the context of your belief system (or your projected mental overlay) at that moment, whether waking or dreaming.

Barrett's study does not surprise experienced lucid dreamers, who have seen projected mental overlay in action and know that levels of lucid awareness exist. In Ed Kellogg's continuum of levels, beyond the state of lucid awareness comes fully lucid and then super-lucid awareness, in which you do possess a clear memory of your waking-life details, realize that a mental realm seems best manipulated with mental powers, see through limiting mental overlay, and properly assess the nature of your situation to a high degree. In her research, Barrett confirms the tendency for more experienced lucid dreamers to act more aware of relating to dream figures, dream objects, and a mental realm, indifferent to waking-life physics.

Setting Up Experiments

Because of the dynamic nature of lucid dreaming (which can reflect your belief system back to you), you must take care in conducting experiments. For this reason, it seems better to create the full outline of your experiment and procedures in the waking physical state, and possibly with assistance from experienced lucid dreamers. Awake, you can examine the experimental process carefully and avoid possible flaws and commonly perceived limitations that lucid dreamers report, like the difficulty of remembering large amounts of data.

Experienced lucid dreamers can point out difficulties with an experiment, like having multiple tasks to perform in the dream. Besides the difficulty in remembering all the tasks, keeping the responses straight, and then waking with that information, you may find multiple tasks too time consuming. An experiment may emerge in which you feel predisposed to doubt the premise and the possibility of achieving any results.

In the German research on dream figures and their ability to solve math problems, the lucid dreamer who continued to perform the experiment after the research had ended reported that the later set of dream figures did better. Does this show that the lucid dreamer worked through their disbelief, or did a more accepting mindset allow for more capable dream figures? Sometimes, even the nature of your belief system needs consideration before an experiment begins, because if you doubt the experiment's possibility, it can affect your actions and approach. For best results, review the experiment and work out these issues while awake.

On occasions when you find yourself in a lucid dream and then try to create an experiment and procedures, your assumptions and beliefs can sometimes fail to address common concerns of scientific protocol (verifiability, measurement, and so on). Although you may get results, upon waking, you may realize that the spontaneous experiment had major flaws that tend to limit or invalidate those results. For these reasons, all lucid dreamers need to think deeply about experiments and explorations while awake, before conducting them in lucid dreams.

Here are some helpful suggestions for lucid dreamers who wish to conduct personal experiments:

- Agree to be completely honest with yourself about the lucid event and the results.

- Treat the experiment with sincere curiosity. Open up to it. Make note of any belief-system conflicts.

- Make specific and exact records upon waking. Avoid assumptions. Describe things clearly, particularly the exact wording of your expressed intent within the lucid dream and the response.

- Prepare a thoughtful experimental task before lucid dreaming. Try to avoid multi-stage, complex experiments or ones that involve lots of memorization.

- When you get a response to your experimental objective, wake up immediately with the results. Write them down while they are fresh in your memory.

- Practice your experiments and develop a track record. Look at a history of your experimental results and see your overall level of accuracy.

- Realize that carrying information from the lucid dreaming state to the waking state can be problematic—sometimes plagued by false awakenings, information overload, cryptic symbolic responses, memory limitations, and so on. As you practice, develop your skills.

Interpreting your experimental results holds an entirely new set of issues. We encourage you to see the results of your experiments on a continuum of accuracy. Why? Some experiments lead to yes-or-no answers; either you get it right or you don't. However, let's say that you decide in a lucid dream to ask a broad question that elicits a broad or symbolic response. What then? How do you gauge the experiment's success or failure? Even when Dmitri Mendeleev dreamed of seeing the periodic table of elements, he still made a few adjustments to what he recalled from the dream state.

Upon waking from your lucid dream and writing your report, ask yourself whether you feel that the information seems reliable, clear, and understandable. Did you feel any conflict or uncertainty when conducting the experiment or in the answer's materialization?

The stories of communication pioneers like Bell and Marconi remind us that new discoveries sometimes require considerable work before they overcome resistance and achieve a high degree of ease, practicality, and fidelity. In other words, new communication systems take time to perfect. Although lucid dreaming can function as an inner communication system without wires, tubes, or transistors, the clarity of lucid dreaming communication may need inner adjustments that modulate less tangible items like the lucid dreamer's inner clarity of beliefs, expectations, and intent.

For example, in the history of fiber-optic communication, the industry's future hinged on a process to enhance the purity of the fiber-optic cable. Without a highly pure cable, the information became refracted or distorted by the impurities. After the developers achieved an efficient method to ensure purity, communication by light traveling through fiber-optic cable became a reality around the world.

So in your lucid dream experiments, be sure to examine yourself. See how conflicting beliefs, negative expectations, and divided intents all act as inner impurities that fill inner types of communication with static and discord. As a lucid dream explorer, it helps to clarify your thoughts, beliefs, expectations, and intent. If these are sufficiently clear, the inner communication will be clearer.

Chapter 11

EMOTIONAL HEALING IN LUCID DREAMS

Some psychotherapists report successfully using lucid dreams to combat the recurring nightmares from post-traumatic stress disorder (PTSD). In chapter 1, you read the story of Hope, who lost her leg in a work-related accident and overcame recurring nightmares by becoming lucidly aware. As Hope mentioned, and various psychotherapists have confirmed, becoming lucid just once during a recurring nightmare often leads to a virtual cessation of the debilitating dreams. PTSD sufferers can thus regain a more normal sleep time. But does lucid dreaming offer psychology anything more when it comes to enhancing emotional health?

If you talk to experienced lucid dreamers, it definitely appears so. In this chapter, we share the stories of some lucid dreamers who use this state to bring forth emotional healing. By sharing these stories, we hope to encourage the field of psychology to see both the healing potential of lucid dreaming and its ability to map the inner realms of the psyche.

Taming the Monsters

A Norwegian woman, Line Salvesen, seems a truly unique and phenomenal lucid dreamer. Every year, she has more than 1,000 lucid dreams. She represents one of those rare individuals who become lucid a few times each night. In her case, she believes that nightmares taught her to become lucid when very young.

Most of my first lucid dreams were triggered by fear during nightmares, so the first thing I learned was how to wake myself up. I did that a lot during my first couple of years or so as a lucid dreamer [in response to the nightmares]. . . . When my realizations grew, I managed to face my dream monsters now and then, and I asked them to be my friends and play.

Even in those early years, Line realized that playing and making friends with her dream monsters seemed a much better response than fighting, denying, or hiding.[100] Currently, some lucid dreaming parents report teaching their young children who complain of nightmares to try to befriend the scary figures—or, better yet, become consciously aware and see whether they want to play. Children often learn how to become lucid and befriend these inner aspects when they are told: "You only see the monster when dreaming, right? So the next time you see the monster, remind yourself that you must be dreaming. Ask the monster if it wants to be your friend and play with you."

As an adult, Line began to realize that some claimed to use lucid dreaming for very practical purposes, like overcoming recurring nightmares or PTSD and ending lifelong phobias. She contacted Robert and asked whether he thought lucid dreaming could end her intense fear of flying. She asked, hoping that she could fly to an International Association for the Study of Dreams conference in the coming year.

Robert knew that Line had wonderful skills as a lucid dreamer, so he encouraged her to try the following. When she became lucid and remembered her interest in overcoming her fear of flying, he recommended that she go to a dream airport and, if she felt okay, get on an airplane (knowing it as a lucid dream object). Then, if she wished, she should stay on the plane until it took off and see how she felt emotionally while flying in it.

Although it involved a lucid dream plane, the experience seemed real to Line on many levels. The flight attendants looked like real flight attendants; the seats felt like real airplane seats; the rumble of takeoff felt much like a real plane taking off. Experiencing this in the virtual reality of the lucid dream state could produce a sense of familiarity and acceptance, which might begin to resolve the phobia. In addition, at almost any time, Line could stop or conclude the experience by waking up.

Line reports that it took her a number of months to achieve her goal. At first, becoming lucid and visiting an airport or getting on an airplane resulted in a bit of anxiety, but she decided to just continue and see what it was like. As she became more comfortable, she found it easier to get on dream planes and fly on them. At one point, she recalls affirming in a lucid dream: "I love airplanes!" And then: "I also love airports!" This announcement helped establish these new feelings in her mind.[101]

This lucid dream action seems similar to the process of desensitization or graduated exposure therapy in psychology. For example, a person with a fear of snakes may be gradually exposed to them by a psychologist to overcome the fear. At first, it may be a photo of a small snake. At the next session, photos of larger snakes are presented. Then gradually, over many weeks or months, a toy rubber snake may be introduced that the person actually touches. Finally, the person is encouraged to become comfortable around physical snakes.

It appears that lucid dreaming allows for a new type of desensitization, inasmuch as lucid dreamers can realistically engage fear on multiple sensory levels in the virtual reality of the lucid dream. Moreover, they can sense any emotions that may arise and determine if or when to conclude the experience. Sometimes, along with the felt emotions, new intuitional understandings or "ah-ha moments" of realization may arise, which occasionally happen in lucid dreams.

In the realm of lucid dreaming, you may hear stories of some who use this ability to overcome various fears—the fear of public speaking or a fear of heights, for example. For many, the primary issue involves understanding the concept of emotional healing in lucid dreams and then learning how to approach it in a thoughtful manner. Unfortunately, little attention has been paid to the practical application of lucid dreaming for emotional healing, although the potential seems enormous.

Although studies show that deep sleep is a time of physical restoration and renovation, REM and dreaming are times for memory encoding and emotional regulation.[102] When people are deprived of REM sleep, it is typically their emotional well-being that suffers most.[103] Dreams sometimes contain emotional content and issues, which may have been suppressed and may seek resolution. This makes dreams a perfect arena for revealing the source of emotional issues and a fertile ground for healing.

Healing and Transformation

A lucid dreamer whom we'll call James reports using lucid dreams to heal emotionally from an issue that was affecting him deeply. As an adult, he had a desire to do volunteer work with children in hospices and possibly become a therapist. Yet he noticed that he became very depressed when he was around children with severe disabilities. This distressed him, and he sought to understand his reaction.

With the aid of reflective meditation, James identified that being around children with severe learning disabilities brought up some repressed emotions from his childhood. As a child, he had had surgery and, as a result, repeatedly visited the hospital for checkups. He recalls sitting anxiously in the waiting room for what seemed like hours, along with children who had severe disabilities. He realized that, while nervously waiting for the doctor, he had associated these children and their disabilities with his feeling of anxiety.

As a lucid dreamer, James wondered whether lucid dreaming could help him work through these anxious emotions. He began by making the intention before falling asleep to become aware that he was dreaming and meet the denied and repressed parts of himself. Doing this led to three lucid dreams that he feels affected him deeply and resolved this emotional issue.

Dream 1: I was walking home. I was following a three-legged dog. As I neared my house, the dog changed into a huge black monster with glaring blue eyes. I wasn't scared and realized it was a dream. I said thank you to the dream.

Dream 2: I was lucid in a room that seemed to have no ceiling. There were two people there who appeared to be my friends. They were talking really loud, almost shouting at me, telling me how much of a bad person I was. I focused on my breathing, sat down, and started meditating. Slowly I started floating sideways and then passed through the wall.

Dream 3: There were kids playing football in a grassy courtyard. It felt like I was at school. The ball came to me and I kicked it, but the wind took it and it landed back at my feet. Everyone jeered at me because I couldn't kick a ball properly. I walked away but had a feeling one of them was following me. I became lucid as I turned and saw him following me. I realized he was an aspect of myself, so I went to him and hugged him. I woke up.

In the first dream, when James becomes lucid, he lets go of reactive fear and simply thanks his awareness for bringing it to his attention. In the next two dreams, he apparently encounters other disowned aspects of himself, but decides to respond differently—by meditating in the second dream (which symbolically lets him rise above it) and by hugging and accepting the jeering self-aspect in the third.

James reports that he has now been able to pursue his aspiration to play music in a therapeutic environment and credits the lucid dreams.

> Since these dreams, I have started volunteering at a children's hospice. I am running music relaxation sessions for the patients and caregivers. After my first session, I sat in my car and was amazed to realize that there were no negative feelings arising in me whatsoever. I felt normal, calm, happy. It seems that a combination of retrospective meditation, making the connection from my childhood and revisiting it, and the shadow work in my [lucid] dreams has changed something. Something massive.

James felt his lucid dreams allowed him to explore shadow work. Jung believed that we each have a shadow composed of the parts of ourselves we reject, repress, or deny. Often when a person experiences something negative, according to the Jungian approach, he may fail to process the experience and associated emotions, which end up as repressed or denied energy in the psyche. Although the person may not be aware of it consciously, the emotional reaction now exists at an unconscious level and may emerge during waking life, especially at certain times (like when James, as an adult, saw disabled children).

Jung felt that dreams occasionally bring up shadow elements that seek some kind of expression or recognition. Often, nightmarish or repulsive figures can be interpreted as shadow elements in the Jungian sense. By embracing these denied or forgotten parts of the self and reintegrating them consciously, transformation occurs, according to therapists and dream workers. The word *healing* literally means "making whole." In this sense, shadow work is a process of identifying the parts of the self that have been rejected and reintegrating them with the hope of making the psyche complete and whole once more.

Emotional Well-Being and Physical Health

People often learn from family and society to suppress certain emotions. Some emotions are harder to feel than others, and some are considered less acceptable or uglier than others. In this chapter and the next, we see how powerfully belief affects our physical condition. The medical profession has tended to downplay the relationship between physical symptoms and emotional issues, but many healthcare professionals are now treating emotional causes of physical illness more seriously. Physicians like Andrew Weil suggest that, rather than suppressing symptoms, our bodies' innate mechanisms for healing can be nurtured and allowed to flourish.[104] Stress and other emotional factors can suppress the immune system and the body's natural healing mechanisms.

The power of emotional issues to initiate or prolong physical illness may be vastly underestimated. Edward Tick, in his book *The Practice of Dream Healing,* mentions a successful cardiologist who decided to go back to medical school to retrain as a psychotherapist. He stated: "I realized that only ten percent of my patients had any physiological heart disease, while ninety percent of all the heart complaints I treated were emotionally or psychologically based. I had to change my specialty to the mind in order to treat illnesses of the heart effectively."[105]

Many in the field of psychology believe that whatever we suppress has a habit of expressing itself in our dreams. Suppressed emotional issues may appear in our dreams in a literal or in a symbolic way. Of course, lucid dreaming provides a new and profound opportunity for processing suppressed emotional content. Sometimes having enough awareness to understand what is being suppressed is sufficient to instigate healing, because the waking self now understands and can assist. At other times, fully acknowledging and expressing suppressed feelings or emotions within a lucid dream seems in itself a powerful relief and a healing act. An example of the apparent physical effect of releasing suppressed emotion in lucid dreaming appears in the following case of lucid dream healing.

Caz Coronel, music producer, DJ, and lucid dreaming teacher, sought to rid herself of persistent tinnitus and felt that repressed emotions might underlie it. Caz suffered specifically from hearing-loss tinnitus, which she experienced as a consistent ringing in the ears. According to medical theory, the brain, in clever response to a tone it can no longer hear, re-creates exactly the same tone that the ear has lost the ability to detect, generating a phantom sound. The problem occurs when the brain generates that tone constantly and persistently. It is enough to drive people mad, and cases have been reported of people committing suicide because they cannot bear it.

After researching the condition thoroughly, Caz tried various approaches to heal it, but in vain. She felt driven to despair:

> I couldn't sleep let alone live with this God-awful noise. After months of freaking out, seriously considering chopping off my head and failing to find any solution, I realized I had no choice but to surrender to it. The tinnitus was here to stay, and there was no cure and no escaping it. Five years passed, and the tinnitus had well established itself. . . .[106]

While exploring alternatives, Caz read that some people felt these symptoms may sometimes be due to repressed emotion. She felt that, although the initial trigger had been the use of headphones in her work as a DJ, the persistence of the tinnitus might have underlying emotional triggers. In a lucid dream, she decided to explore that idea. The dream begins in a garden, when she becomes lucid.

> I turn to CJ and say, "The pond looks wonderful like this, all the life has come back to it." Then suddenly I realize something. "Hey, there is no pond in my garden anymore. This is a lucid dream!" "Oh yeah!" CJ says, as if she really already knew but was indulging me. Suddenly I remember my purpose to heal my suppressed pain. I shout out to the dream, "I need a guru!" But then I realize that isn't going to work. I reason with myself—I've made that mistake before; no one can heal you but you. What I need is my higher self, I need myself! I then call out to the dream, "I want to

feel my unrepressed pain" (meaning I want to feel my pain unrepressed). Suddenly my body starts to hurt a lot all over and it is hard to move. Everyone else in the garden becomes frozen and my mouth starts to seal over so I can no longer speak (like Neo's mouth in the film *The Matrix*). I can barely open it, as hard as I try. I feel completely inhibited to express myself.

"I don't need to put up with this!" I think. Suddenly I launch myself at my frozen friends. I give them all a giant hug, sending them all the love I have.[107]

Caz woke from the lucid dream with a thumping heart. When she listened, the tinnitus was gone. "I was ecstatic, jumping around and phoning everyone I knew whom I could talk to about it," she recalls. "Now many months have passed and it still hasn't returned; I am truly grateful!"

This interesting example illustrates the potential of lucid dreaming for consciously understanding and using the unconscious for waking benefit. Caz's story shows that lucid dreaming may be used to explore emotional issues and, in this case, the connection between emotions and physical healing. When Caz breaks free at the end of the lucid dream, she seeks to express her positive emotion of love to those around her. This may suggest the importance of free expression and expressing love as ingredients to our more complete physical and emotional well-being.

Red Dreams

To pursue her healing journey further, Caz chose to incubate a red dream, inspired by a Mexican Toltec dreaming practice that involves returning to the womb in the dream state, which this tradition considers one of the most powerfully healing dream experiences. Mexican Toltecs believe that red dreams can have emotional, as well as physical, restorative effects.

Caz sought out these red dreams while lucidly aware on a few occasions. She felt transported back into her mother's womb and recalls an overwhelming yet profound sense of peace there. She had a very real sense of her small, embryonic body and her tiny hands. She reports seeing, in great and realistic detail, the blood vessels surrounding her.

Amazingly, she also had a very real feeling of being contained in the safety of the amniotic sac (suggestive of prenatal memory).

These lucid dreams resulted in a sense of awe at being carried and held by her mother's body for nine months. Caz didn't always feel nurtured by their relationship in waking life, but here in these lucid red dreams, she felt a sense of what her mother had given her. The lucid dream experience reminded her that she would not exist without this gift of life from her mother. Not surprisingly, these dreams have allowed healing feelings of compassion and forgiveness to emerge more strongly in their relationship. Caz reports that these dreams have had a profoundly healing effect on her emotional self and left her more at peace.

A Cautionary Note

Lucid dreaming does not guarantee success, ensure well-being and health, or imply wisdom. Like any tool, it should be used thoughtfully and with respect. When Robert speaks to university classrooms, he often announces a basic guideline: "If you find waking life really difficult, then leave lucid dreaming alone. Concentrate on creating a constructive waking life first, before seeking to lucid dream."

Although no official guidelines exist, lucid dreaming does not seem appropriate for those suffering deep depression, feelings of dissociation, or mental illness. Further, lucid dreaming should not be used to replace professional care. Please consult your therapist or physician if you have any condition that causes concern.

A Simple Path to Vibrant Health

Lucid dreaming is an amazing tool for bringing your conscious awareness into contact with your unconscious for greater integration and illumination. The previous examples give helpful clues to how lucid dreamers have used this state to overcome recurring nightmares, significant phobias, debilitating reactions, and perhaps emotional blockages.

Elsewhere in the book, we have noted that lucid dreaming often shows the power of belief and expectation, as well as the power of unthinking projections. With practice, lucid dreaming can bring greater awareness of your inner life, and this, in and of itself, may serve as the simplest path to vibrant health.

In this section, we can only offer general observations about the possible use of lucid dreaming for improving emotional well-being, and even these may not be suitable to all situations. In general, however, take things gradually. Become comfortable with the lucid dream environment before tackling big issues. Play. Have fun. Fly around and create things. See how the lucid dream environment responds and how your thoughts, beliefs, expectations, and feelings are reflected in the scene around you.

Then, when you feel comfortable in lucid dreams, note the areas in your dreams that have the most energy. This energy may express itself as a lot of activity, as in building a house or welcoming a newly crowned queen. Follow the activity as a careful observer, noting any thoughts that come to mind. The highest energy levels may also be expressed as disagreements, arguments, or more. Again, observe these; but also note how you feel about coming to this kind of energy. Does it appeal to you? Worry you? Interest you?

How to Improve Your Health and Well-Being

You do not need to become lucid to use the sleep and dream states to improve your sense of health and well-being. For example, consider this simple practice.

Before sleep, repeat this suggestion: "Tonight while I am sleeping, my body will be restored to its natural health and vibrant condition, and I will wake feeling refreshed and energized." When you do this before sleep, it helps make your intent very clear in your mind, perhaps allowing it to percolate into your subconscious to affect dream content. It may not matter whether you remember your dreams that night; the important thing is that you have suggested a clear intent and note how you feel in the morning. If successful, you should feel surprisingly refreshed and energized.

||||||||||||||||||||||||||||||||||||||||||||||||||||||||||||||||||||||||||||||||||||||||||||||||||||||||||||||||||||||||||||||||||||||||||||||||||||||||||||||||||||||||

The energy in a dream comes in many forms—objects, settings, and figures. On average, if the energy seems largely constructive, supportive, or neutral, it suggests that you have no major issues requiring immediate attention. However, if you find yourself lucidly aware and routinely facing difficult situations (like the persistent brick wall in chapter 6), you may need to question the dream symbol or figures to grasp what needs acknowledgement.

If you ever feel that you have met seemingly threatening dream figures, you may wish to send them thoughts of compassion and peace. Often, this leads to an immediate change in the energy to something more peaceful and benign. Lucid dreamers frequently discover that threatening energy simply wants to be understood and accepted on some level. By projecting sincere thoughts of compassion and peace, this understanding and acceptance may occur more rapidly.

Sometimes, you may also be presented with a limiting belief or personal aspect of yourself that seeks resolution. The limiting belief may involve needing rented wings to fly well; the personal aspect may be a discarded aspect that seeks complete acceptance. If you can open up to these situations thoughtfully, you stand to gain new insights and energy.

Finally, lucid dreaming can bring up the unexpected and surprising. You may meet a cyclops from Greek myth, a talking horse, a deceased grandparent, or robed monks. Note the lucidity or awareness in these figures. See them as opportunities to learn and grow and, in some cases, heal emotionally. When you are aware of being aware, the potential for making progress seems exponential—if you open to the moment.

Chapter 12

INTENDING PHYSICAL HEALTH

Writer, artist, and lucid dreamer Maria Isabel Pita was playing catch-the-stick with a puppy when she fell, breaking her fall with both hands. Days later, she felt excruciating pain in her right wrist and thumb, so severe that she felt forced to use only her left hand. The condition did not improve, even though she wore a brace and tried numerous external aids. The doctor said that she had developed tendonitis and felt concerned that it might become a chronic condition.

Seeing no improvement after several weeks, Maria decided to try to heal herself in her next lucid dream.[108] She recalls this dream:

> I find myself fully conscious of being awake in a dream where I'm lying on my back on my bed in our bedroom, which is dark. I raise my right hand toward the ceiling thinking, "Make light," and violet sparkles emanate from my fingertips, which delight me, and also succeed in gently illuminating the ceiling, where a circular decorative carving has replaced our actual ceiling fan. I notice then that my right hand is wearing the cloth brace I've been subjected to for weeks now because of a strained tendon. (Yesterday it was worse than ever; I couldn't move my thumb in any direction without pain shooting through me, so that I was obliged to skip yoga, which really upset me.) At once, I remember my intent. Raising both hands before me, I point the index finger of my left hand at the junction of my right wrist and thumb, willing a healing energy into it. I'm

delighted to see a stream of lovely blue and violet sparkles. (I can't think of better word for them.)

I then take the time to remove the cloth brace so it won't be in the way and direct the starry healing energy to just above the tender area. At one point, I can't see anything, but I'm aware of lying in bed having this lucid dream and of struggling to disconnect the desire to open my eyes in the dream with [sic] the urge to open my actual physical eyes, which will wake me up. I don't know how I manage it, perhaps through sheer willpower, but I find myself once again gazing at the dream room and my hands.

I turn my right hand so I can see the bottom of my wrist and trace my left index finger along it. I can see beneath the skin; a section of skin seems to be missing. I discern a black line or band of sorts, which at first looks like an inverted syringe with something sharp and dark moving up my arm from my wrist. I'm quite fascinated to be seeing the inside of my body as I continue directing healing energy that consists of a shimmering violet light indistinguishable from my intent, which is the real mysterious source of the "corrective" power I'm focusing on my wrist and thumb. I become aware of a golden light slightly behind me to my left and give thanks for this dream as it slowly fades and I find myself awake in bed.

Upon waking, Maria removed the cloth brace and found she could move her wrist and thumb in different directions without any pain. In her dream journal, she wrote:

If I have to assign a percentage to the improvement in my condition, I would say seventy-five percent. My wrist also feels *so* much stronger, nowhere near as weak and vulnerable to being accidentally moved in the wrong direction. It's very interesting how connected I feel to this part of my body after seeing it in the dream, and seeing *into* it.

Years later, she reports that the tendonitis completely disappeared, and her wrist and hand feel perfectly fine.

The Body's Response to Dreams

Anyone who wakes from a nightmare with heart thumping and breathing rapid naturally knows that dream content can create a physical response. To some degree, the body responds to dreams as if what we are dreaming is happening. According to Professor Robert Haskell: "Dreaming is a real physiological event. Whatever is dreamed is real in terms of physiological responses."[109]

Hormones, endorphins, and neurotransmitters can be released in response to dream content. Heart rate, nervous system response, respiration, and body temperature can all be affected. Neural pathways and brain regions relating to the dream's content become active.[110] These are all responses that have a very real impact on the physical body.

The practice of lucid dream healing thus seems a natural outgrowth of the scientific research conducted by Stephen LaBerge. In numerous studies, LaBerge gathered evidence that a lucid dream event has a corresponding effect on the physical body. For example, when lucid dream eyes move, it results in a corresponding movement in the physical eyes. So too, when a dream hand clenches, it results in a tightening of forearm muscles to some degree. He even conducted one set of sleep-lab experiments in which a lucid dreamer was instructed to have lucid dream sex, so that sixteen physiologic measurements could be taken and compared to the physiology of waking sex. Again, the results found a striking correspondence in the physical body's response to lucid dream sex on almost every physical measure.[111] For the body, a lucid dream event sometimes seems almost as powerful in creating corresponding bodily changes as the real thing.

Indeed, almost every issue of *Lucid Dreaming Experience* receives a submission or two reporting apparent physical healing through a lucid dream. In the most recent issue,[112] a lucid dreamer reports having a chronic gastrointestinal ailment. In two lucid dreams, he focuses healing light on his abdomen and reports that, thereafter, the problems diminished substantially. Another reports having difficulty recovering from surgery because another illness and hospital stay followed it. Then in a lucid dream, she recalls her intent to heal from the original surgery. A very large man agrees to assist her and offers her a glowing rod of light, which she places on her dream body, intending it to heal. Three weeks later, she goes to her scheduled post-op checkup and the doctor reports a complete recovery.

The journal, *Medical Hypotheses*, reported an interesting example of lucid dream healing in their article, "Chronic Pain Resolution after a lucid dream: A case for neural plasticity?"[113] In the abstract, the authors explain the situation and their hypotheses, "Using as a model the unique case of Mr. S, a patient suffering with chronic pain for 22 years who experienced a complete resolution of pain after a lucid dream following 2 years of biopsychosocial treatments, we postulate that central nervous system (CNS) reorganization (i.e., neural plasticity) serves as a possible mechanism for the therapeutic benefit of multidisciplinary treatments, and may set a neural framework for healing, in this case via a lucid dream." After 22 years of chronic pain, you can easily imagine the relief that Mr. S feels after resolving this in a lucid dream. The point that the biopsychosocial treatments may have created a "neural framework for healing" seems significant, since lucid dreamers often note the importance of a supportive belief system.

Knowing that scientific research confirms that the body responds to dream content makes it easier to accept the idea of physical healing in a lucid dream. When you read the successful accounts of lucid dreamers who apparently accomplished healing by consciously intending it, their actions seem to parallel the scientific reports of dream content resulting in subsequent body response. However, for some people, conceptual barriers exist. They can accept that a lucid dream may affect a dreamer's emotional state, muscle or eye movement, and even swimming ability. But influencing the body for physical healing seems a conceptual barrier.

The Placebo Effect

If lucid dreamers naturally affect their physical bodies to some noticeable degree (moving eyes, altering muscles, changing respiration), then strongly focused intent toward healing should affect the body toward healing to some noticeable degree (reduction in the severity of symptoms, more rapid healing, constructive change in the ailment, and so on). Lucid dreamers' experiences suggest that healing seems to result from strongly focused intent consciously directed while aware in the dream state.

In the waking state, strongly focused belief and expectation has shown a dramatic ability to influence the body. A wealth of research has followed, uncovering how our thoughts and behavior affect different mechanisms of the body, like hormones, neurotransmitters, and neural pathways. Thoughts and behaviors have even been shown to affect the nervous system, the size of different brain structures, and, amazingly, the expression of our DNA.[114]

Consider the placebo effect. A placebo is simply an inert substance like a sugar pill that the recipient believes to be some form of treatment for a condition or illness. Placebos frequently create both physical and psychological healing responses, even though there is no active substance in the placebo itself. The response is purely psychological or psychosomatic. For decades, the placebo effect has been widely recognized and used as a control to test the effectiveness of new treatments and medicines.

One fascinating case illustrating how profoundly a placebo can affect the body's ability to heal comes from a patient in 1957. Mr. Wright was dying of lymphatic cancer, with tumors the size of oranges. He had been told he had just days to live. He heard about a new drug being tested—Krebiozen. Believing this might be his last hope, he asked his doctor to give it to him. His physician agreed to grant what he thought was a dying wish. "I had left him febrile [feverish], gasping for air, completely bedridden," the doctor said. However, two days later, "the tumor masses had melted like snowballs on a hot stove, and in only these few days they were half their original size! . . . Within 10 days, he was able to be discharged from his deathbed, practically all signs of his disease having vanished."[115]

Unfortunately, after this recovery, news reports started to emerge stating the poor results of Krebiozen in clinical studies on test patients. After two months of almost perfect health, Wright, disturbed by these new reports, relapsed rapidly to his original state and became very depressed. His doctor, hoping to re-create the initial healing response, told him that a greatly improved version of Krebiozen had now been developed and offered to administer a doubly potent preparation. In fact, he injected Wright with *fresh water and nothing more*. Once again, the patient experienced a placebo response that was nothing short of miraculous. His lungs cleared, his tumors vanished, and he was once again fully active. Devastatingly, the American Medical Association then released its official statement on Krebiozen, declaring it worthless in the treatment of cancer. Once again, Wright relapsed; he died shortly thereafter.[116]

This phenomenon, researched in innumerable studies, *provides convincing evidence* that the mind can play a significant role in the physical healing process. Specifically, it shows precisely what lucid dreamers have discovered when operating in the unconscious of dreaming: Positive expectation and belief properly focused on a desired intent can create astounding inner changes that radiate outward to affect the body, the emotions, and the psyche.

Likewise, studies using deep hypnosis have shown the effectiveness of using focused suggestions inserted in the subconscious to alleviate many physical symptoms, including asthma, irritable bowel syndrome, warts, eczema, psoriasis, and hives.[117] However, only a relatively small percentage of the population is capable of entering a deep hypnotic state—called the somnambulistic state—which is where the most effective healing occurs. In lucid dreaming, on the other hand, your waking awareness has already made it to a deep state and, once there, has the capacity to focus healing intent actively toward emotional and physical ailments.

Healing in Lucid Dreams

As I (Caroline) was writing this chapter, some nasty colds were going around in London, and I managed to fall victim to one of them. I had a particularly sore throat one morning and wanted to see whether I could soothe it in a lucid dream. I fell directly into a lucid dream from waking and instantly shouted to the dream: "Please heal my throat. Thank you. My throat is healed!" I began to float upward, and about a dozen or so effervescent white balls of light appeared. The dream scene dissolved into formless radiant light, and I could feel a serenely blissful energy radiating from the orbs through my entire body. I was suddenly woken by a noise outside. I fought coming back, but was unable to stay in the dream.

Upon waking, I instantly noticed that I had absolutely no pain in my throat (or at least no perception of pain). However, I still had all the other symptoms of the cold. Needless to say, I regretted limiting my intent to healing only my throat. The experience couldn't have lasted much more than a few minutes, but it reminded me of the importance of clarifying my intentions. In a lucid dream, your verbal requests and suggestions will often be manifested very literally. Take time to think about what you want to ask for and phrase it thoughtfully. Realize that asking to heal your throat will likely result in a different outcome than asking to heal your cold.

In successful cases of lucid dream healing, dreamers have shared certain characteristics. First, they acted directly to achieve healing. For example, they acted to create a ball of healing light, or placed healing energy in their dream hands, or focused positive affirming thoughts of healing onto an affected area. Their focus, expectation, and dream action all aligned and led to successful lucid dream healing experiences. Second, they believed in the possibility of healing their ailments in a lucid dream.

Contrast this with a case in which a lucid dreamer did not achieve healing. In this case, the dreamer became lucid, but then decided to find a dream doctor to heal her. When she finally found a doctor and asked for healing, the doctor replied: "I'm tired. It's late. And you always come here on Fridays." Throughout the lucid dream, the doctor and a nurse suggested that the dreamer should eat certain foods, but she always refused their suggestions. By the end of the dream, she screamed at the doctor to come back and help her, but he did not. When she awoke, her condition showed no change.[118]

From this simple example, an important lesson in lucidity emerges. Sadly, this dreamer sought someone to heal her in a lucid dream instead of acting to heal her own ailment directly. She apparently believed that someone else must do the healing.

You can use these examples and lessons to your advantage. If you have an ailment, pre-plan a lucid dream healing experience. In your plan, determine how you will act directly on yourself in the lucid dream. The preceding stories show various types of direct action, which you can use as examples to emulate. These waking plans will help you recall your intent and how to act when you become lucid.

As a lucid dream experimenter, you can use your creativity, intuition, and inventiveness to explore the mind's ability to affect the physical body for better health. But, with any health situation, you should investigate and use all medical aids at your disposal. The concept of lucid dreaming should be viewed as experimental and a possible adjunct in support of your traditional medical approach. For those curious about experimenting personally, we suggest that you first think about your intent and how to accomplish it. Most people's intent will be curative, but some will focus on diagnostic help or prescriptive needs.

How to Heal in a Lucid Dream

Once lucid within a dream, try one or more of the following to engage your intent to cure:

- Send healing light to the wound, disease, or injured area by either creating a ball of light between your hands or intending light to emerge from your hands onto the ailment.

- Announce a predetermined chant to focus your energies (e.g., "Now from my hands with power divine, the healing light on my knee will shine!") or sing a mantra or sound that you feel encourages healing.

- Announce a positive healing affirmation (e.g., "Thank you, my knee is healed!")

- With your mind, invest something with healing energy (e.g., your hands) and then place it on the affected area.

- Conjure a dream medicine, which you infuse with healing intent.

If you have a physical issue you are attempting to heal in a lucid dream, try following the advice of Charlie Morley, London-based author and lucid dreaming teacher—include a suggestion that affirms that *the ailment is healed*. After expressing your healing intent in the lucid dream, affirmatively suggest that the healing has happened. For example, after Maria shines light on her ailing wrist and thumb, she could announce: "My wrist and thumb are healed!" Also, feel free to express your gratitude to your body, the dream, and larger awareness. Gratitude often creates a feedback loop bringing us the future experience of more gratitude.

Finally, experienced lucid dreamers sometimes report receiving inner guidance or suggestions when seeking to heal themselves. If you get inner information, allow it to guide your experience.

The beauty of lucid dreaming is that it allows for personal and scientific experimentation. Although medical researchers have yet to explore lucid dreaming as an alternative means for healing, many lucid dreamers have decided to conduct personal experiments, often with surprisingly positive results. We look forward to the day when potential uses of lucid dreaming like emotional and physical healing receive the scientific attention that they deserve.

Until that time, feel free to submit your lucid dreams of successful or unsuccessful healing experiences to magazines like *Lucid Dreaming Experience*. Gathering a record of case reports may be the first step in bringing needed attention to this important area.

Chapter 13

MEDITATING IN LUCID DREAMS

What happens when you meditate in a lucid dream?

When I (Caroline) first attempted to meditate in a lucid dream, I had been practicing meditation in my waking life for several years. Discovering meditation was life-changing. I felt happier and more self-disciplined, and I made better life decisions. When I meditate in the waking state, I first focus on my breath, allowing it to slow. By observing and connecting with my breath, I can sink into the present moment. My focus turns inward and, within me, I feel an expansive spaciousness and a sense of timeless, infinite peace. Some days, it takes me a while to let go of distractions and I battle with mind chatter; on other days, it seems effortless.

A couple of years ago, I became curious about meditating in lucid dreams. The idea of combining two empowering activities like meditating and lucid dreaming filled me with curiosity and excitement! One morning, I found myself in a dream surrounded by a vivid green field of lush grass. I questioned the dreamlike color of the grass, which was so green that it appeared surreal and vibrant. I then realized I was dreaming. I touched the grass beneath my feet, running my fingers through the soft blades, allowing the tactile sensations to help stabilize the dream.

I remembered my intention to meditate and sat down cross-legged on the grass. I closed my eyes, started to focus on my breath, and began to direct my attention inward. Before I had even taken a full breath or barely begun to meditate formally, I felt totally engulfed by a sensation of pure bliss. It seemed as if every cell in my body was physically vibrating with transcendent ecstasy. The feeling had such intensity that, within a few moments, I woke up!

I was astounded by the profound energy of the experience. I had never imagined going that deeply into a meditative state so quickly. Even though it was a brief experience, I felt the positive effects long after I woke up, and it left me eager to try again. I have since discovered that, the more I practice meditating in lucid dreams, the easier it is to sustain the state. I have also found that keeping my eyes open helps me prolong the dreaming meditative state. Furthermore, a regular meditation practice in waking life seems to lead me to more success when meditating in a lucid dream.

Of course, there are many ways to meditate. When asking lucid dreamers to share their experiences of lucid dream meditation, I found that even the definition of meditation varies from person to person. Some perform *Vipassana* meditation; some simply focus on a single point of awareness; some empty their minds; some focus on breathing techniques; some meditate by chanting mantras or sacred sounds. Author and Buddhist meditation teacher B. Alan Wallace encourages deep meditative practices of focus and attention leading to *shamatha,* or meditative quiescence. Some lucid dreamers are very precise about their meditation practice, whereas others believe that the intention to meditate is more important than the specific method or technique.

Meditators' experiences in dreams are as varied as their ways of meditating, but consistently, those who meditate within lucid dreams report one or more of the following experiences:

- A state of bliss or ecstasy

- A feeling of transcendence

- Increased energy

- Heightened perception

- Insight into concepts or issues

- Altered perception of time or space

- A deep sense of universal oneness

When meditation is performed in the lucid dream state, you will likely enter meditation deeply and quickly, achieving astonishing states of awareness. In this chapter, we consider a variety of meditating styles and the self-reports of lucid dreamers as we seek to discover what happens when you meditate in lucid dreams.

Breathing and Mantras

Meditation often involves a point of focus like the breath to help the meditator let go of thoughts. John D. Cooper has experimented with Vipassana meditation in lucid dreams—a technique that involves mindful focusing on the breath and feeling into the sensations of the body as a point of focus. Here, he reports a lucid dream in which he meditates:

> I am lying on my bed, yet something does not feel completely real. As I have trained myself to question reality even when awake, I am able to become aware that I'm in a dream, lying on my dream bed. I try to recall [my] various dream tasks, and I decide to meditate. I sit cross-legged and do a Vipassana meditation. . . . I suddenly tumble out of my dream body, like a cloud, rolling upwards. I am filled with pure joy and love. I feel light and free from all suffering. I roll down and land softly beside my dream bed like a snowflake landing on the ground. I start to consider that I have tapped into a higher state of consciousness, and I take the opportunity to ask for wisdom to be downloaded into me. It's as if my egoic need to consume severs the connection with this higher self and at that moment my dream collapses.

John's experience initially illustrates a sense of transcendence and bliss. Interestingly, when his egoic mind tries to take control of the experience at this transcendent level, the lucid dream collapses. From this, you can see that lucid meditation may be cut short by how you choose to respond to the experience. Although your mind may wish to receive some personal objective, the greatest benefit of lucid dream meditation may be simply letting go of thought and sinking into stillness, or just being in that moment.

It can be hard to let go of mind chatter. Some people find it helpful to chant mantras or sacred sounds as a point of focus. Kristen LaMarca has used this approach of chanting in some of her lucid dream meditating experiences. LaMarca wrote about her profound experience of chanting the Aum (or Om) mantra for the first time in a lucid dream:

> Upon realizing I was in a dream, I sat down and placed my palms on my crossed legs as I began to hum the mantra. Without delay, the dreamscape began to reverberate wavelengths that pulsated throughout my body and surroundings. The sound Aum was no longer being produced by my own voice but by the dream itself. Unexpectedly, my arms involuntarily rose over my head into prayer position and then descended toward my heart. My folded hands then raised to my brow and led me to lean forward and place my palms and forehead on the floor, similar to the traditional Islamic prayer position. Aware that I had never before performed or seen this specific motion in my waking life, I continued to observe while attempting to contain my astonishment.[119]

Some people also describe unexpected and beautiful tones coming from their mouths, which they couldn't possibly have produced in waking life. Without breath being a limitation, lucid dreamer Tereza Griffin describes finding to her surprise that she could sustain a single "Om" many, many times longer than would have been possible in waking. In some cases, singing or chanting can result in hearing the sound expressed exponentially in the lucid dream, as if a choir of voices has joined the dreamer. These lucid dreams show how unexpected and surprising developments sometimes occur when you decide to meditate in lucid dreams.

How to Use Mantras and Sacred Sounds

Some traditions feel that certain sounds have a numinous quality or special energy. Try these suggestions to tap into this energy:

- Chant a Sanskrit sound like "Om" (or "Aum"). Some consider this to be the first sound of creation. See what happens in the lucid dream as you focus on making this special sound.

- Chant a Hindu mantra like the Ganesha mantra: "Om Gum Ganapatayei Namaha." In the Hindu tradition, this is believed to remove obstacles and enhance success.

- If you prefer to sing or chant something that is not associated with a belief system, create your own mantra and give it your own intention and meaning. The more you use it, the more your unconscious will associate it with the meaning you give it.

Active Meditation in Lucid Dreams

Some people struggle with sitting meditation practices, yet can more easily achieve a state of mindful focus during active meditation. Eastern practices like yoga, *tai chi*, and *qi gong (chi kung)* can serve as effective active meditations, because they tend to focus your awareness somewhat differently than sitting meditations do.

Dr. Rory Mac Sweeney, a lucid dreaming teacher and former martial arts champion, has experimented with taking tai chi and chi kung practices into the dream state. He sees these as practices leading to present-moment awareness: "Learning to become still behind movement is the essence of the practice." He describes the following experience while lucid in a dream.

There was, during my practice [in the lucid dream], an intense glowing of electric blue light emanating from my hands as I performed my chi kung. An intense presence of being seemed to pervade all of my awareness; it was as if what I was doing was all there was and that no moment other than this could exist. On finishing, I returned to explore the rest of the dream and found that it had a kind of boundless texture to it. I could feel the veil of time had lifted from my awareness. A kind of fearlessness ensued, as I was no longer threatened by the potential loss of my own existence. I pursued the dream for what seemed to be a couple of hours.

Rory feels that, by harmonizing energy in his lucid dream practice using these active meditation techniques, he is able to move closer to stillness and timelessness.

How to Use Active Meditation

Here's an active meditation based on a Taoist chi kung practice. You can use it in either the waking or dreaming state.

- Stand with your feet shoulder-width apart and your knees slightly bent. Make sure your spine is nice and straight. Really *feel* your feet on the floor.

- With your hands in front of you, palms facing toward each other, imagine that you are creating a ball of energy between your hands.

- Make the ball any size you wish. Lucid dreamers may actually perceive a ball of light energy.

- Focus all your attention on the ball and try moving it around, allowing your arms, shoulders, and hips to move and sway, but keeping your feet firmly rooted to the floor.

- When you are ready to end the practice, place the ball of energy in your lower dantian (or *dan t'ien*), which is located just below your navel. In Taoist philosophy, this is considered an important storage center for chi, or life-force energy.

• If lucid dreaming, try putting the ball into different parts of your body and then see what happens. Notice how you feel when you wake.

Meditating in Dream Space

Many people find they can enter a meditative state more quickly and deeply in lucid dreams than they normally do in waking reality. This may be explained in part by the lack of normal bodily distractions in lucid dreaming, which can interfere with meditative focus in waking attempts. LaMarca describes one of her first experiences of meditating in a lucid dream:

> I sat down where I became lucid, closed my eyes, and began to concentrate on my breath. What fascinated me about this experience was how much easier it was to meditate in a lucid dream! I could easily sit up tall and straight without the slightest tinge of discomfort in my lower back. The rewards manifest more immediately as well. I felt as though I was entering some ineffable state of consciousness. I awoke feeling tremendously tranquil, as though I had just completed an hour-long waking meditation in the few minutes I had actually spent in lucid dream meditation.[120]

Clare Johnson, whose doctoral research focused on the link between lucid dreaming and the creative process, has been experimenting with meditation in lucid dreams for over a decade. Like many others, she observes:

> In lucid dream meditation, you go so deep, so fast, it's astonishing. Without the aches and pains and twinges of a physical body, there's no physical distraction, and the mind is focused and clear. My experiences with lucid dream meditation have had a direct and lasting effect on my waking life practice, as it has become much easier for me to switch on

the alert yet relaxed state of mind conducive to meditation, and sink deeply into a meditative state.

The following is an account of one of Clare's early lucid dream meditation experiences.

I'm on the top of a hill with strange granite rock formations. There's a liquid quality to the air and I notice everything as if in slow motion; the pink wildflowers, the prickly grass. I realize this is a dream and smile. I feel strong and fit and climb easily up to the top of the nearest rock and sit down. The dreamscape shimmers with energy and I feel very happy. I'm sitting cross-legged and decide it would be a great place to meditate, so I close my eyes.

All imagery vanishes and it goes black. Instantly I am deeply relaxed, it's so much faster than meditation in the waking state and I marvel at how deep I go within seconds, with no back discomfort or sensory distractions. In fact, I realize I can't feel my dream body at all. I seem to be floating, and I relax and let it happen because I am now in a deep, trancelike state, my thoughts slowing, and it feels right to let go, bit by bit, of "Clare." The darkness is turning to light and as I watch, I become surrounded by and suspended in golden light. It feels so wonderful, like being transformed into radiance, and I want to exclaim in delight but I don't want to lose it, so I just experience this radiance. It no longer seems separate from me; I am the light and it is me, in perfect harmony. The light expands infinitely and I eventually wake up feeling as if I am still bathed in it, refreshed and quiet and peaceful.

Clare has found that, over the past decade, her intention to meditate has become the most important part of her lucid dreaming meditation practice.

As my lucid dream meditation practice has progressed, I don't tend to do the body thing anymore. I used to sit down cross-legged in the dream, straighten my spine, focus on my breath, and so on; in other words, I tried to enter meditation exactly as I would in the waking state. But now when I become lucid in a dream, simply closing my eyes to avoid being distracted by visual imagery and having the strong intention to meditate has the effect of transforming me almost simultaneously into a single point of awareness, like a dot of light. This then often triggers the start of a lucid non-dual experience.

The intention to meditate and the expectation that you will be successful seem important keys for such a powerful experience. As I discovered in my first experience, my intention and focus on meditating seemed much more important than the technical specifics of the meditation method. You may find that intention becomes more important than method. Creating a solid meditation practice in the waking state, however, may allow for greater stability and depth when meditating in a lucid dream.

The Benefits of Meditation

A consistent meditation practice can result in many benefits, including a greater ability to focus in everyday life, reduced stress,[121] a more positive outlook, and a greater sense of well-being. Meditation has been practiced globally in diverse ways in various cultures and in many religions, including Buddhism, Hinduism, Christianity, and Sufism. Its emotional, spiritual, and mental benefits have been widely revered and, in recent years, meditation has been attracting increasing attention in scientific research. Studies have been uncovering a wealth of evidence for its very tangible physical benefits.

The effect of meditation on certain structures of the brain is truly extraordinary. The size and density of structures associated with learning, memory, stress responses, emotional regulation, empathy, and compassion are all affected.[122] It is not just your brain that you change when you meditate; you also tone your nervous system and regulate your blood glucose. You affect your intellect, your health and happiness, and your mental focus, and protect yourself against depression.[123] Meditation has even been shown to help switch on positive genes associated with energy metabolism and switch off genes linked to the body's inflammatory and stress responses.[124] All these physical changes promote mental and physical well-being, deepening your personal experience as well as promoting longevity.[125]

If you do not have a regular meditation practice, there are many meditation techniques you can try, first in waking life, then in your lucid dreams. The practices given here represent just a few. If you are interested in trying more active meditation techniques, enroll in a yoga, tai chi, or chi kung course. Practice the techniques while waking, understand the philosophy behind them, and then re-experience the activity in your lucid dreams.

Everybody is different, so you may need to experiment until you find a meditation style and technique that works for you. Try different meditations when you are awake and set aside some time daily to meditate for at least ten minutes. If you struggle at first, do not worry. Meditation takes practice, but the results are often profoundly rewarding on many levels.

Loving Kindness Meditation

- Sit or lie down in a comfortable position. Either close your eyes or leave them slightly open with your vision not focused on anything in particular.

- Slow your breathing and notice how the air feels as it comes into and leaves your body. Imagine you're taking the breath right into the base of your stomach.

- Allow this connection with your breath to bring you into the present moment; let go of thoughts of the past and thoughts of the future.

- Notice how your body feels and if you are holding any tension anywhere. Breathe into the tension, feeling any anxiety, stress, or tension melt on the inhale and evaporate on the exhale.

- Breathing comfortably, focus your attention into your heart and imagine you are breathing light into it from every direction. Allow the light to fill your heart. Bathe in this light for a while and then see and feel it radiating as an outward expression of love and compassion.

Chapter 14

LIVING LUCIDLY

According to historical accounts, Benjamin Franklin had a deep interest in the science of his time, as in the early investigation of electricity and the use of ballooning. On October 19, 1752, Franklin published his *Letter XI from Benjamin Franklin, Observations on Electricity*, in which he reported on the success of his silk kite experiment in Philadelphia, which succeeded in "drawing electric fire from clouds." You can imagine the excitement of the time as early adopters and researchers began to understand and use the basic principles of electricity. Even lightning, long considered an expression of angry gods, now began to show itself as a natural occurrence based on positive and negative electrical charges in the environment.

Historical accounts suggest that a woman onlooker responded to one of these early experimental demonstrations by disdainfully asking: "Of what use is it?" Benjamin Franklin reportedly answered with a question of his own: "What is the good of a newborn baby?"

As Franklin surmised, the simplistic demonstrations of new discoveries rarely express the profound potential inherent in their nature. Although at first, electricity seemed mainly useful to astonish onlookers with parlor amusements like electrical shocks and bursts of light, electricity and electrical devices eventually showed their transformative potential in changing our daily experience and even our understanding of reality. Because of its fundamental and adaptable nature, our uses for this "newborn baby" continue to grow in depth and complexity even 200 years later.

Lucid dreaming is another discovery with profound potential. Aware in the subconscious, you can maneuver your conscious intent toward almost any goal or endeavor. You can use your lucid awareness for simple amusement and play, or you can also use it to become a better athlete, artist, writer, inventor, teacher, or businessman. Moreover, at this level of the mind, you can use your lucid awareness to explore the very nature of perception, experience, and consciousness itself.

Nevertheless, adopters of any new discovery often bear the burden of getting past existing societal perspectives. Of what use is becoming consciously aware within a dream, particularly when the prevailing culture largely considers dreams synonymous with whimsy and the irrational, with falseness and delusion? Of what use is lucid dreaming if dreams merely show the mind in psychosis or as the random firings of neurons? Of what use is lucid dreaming if dreams have little purpose or value? Why bother dreaming?

You may find comfort in a quote from James Clerk Maxwell, Scottish physicist and father of electromagnetic theory who laid the foundation for Einstein's work: "Thoroughly conscious ignorance is the prelude to every real advance in science." Although research has brought us glimmers of insight, we remain largely ignorant of dreaming, the dream state, and the unconscious. Yet this long-ignored area of dreaming and the unconscious may be where the next real advance in science emerges.

Throughout this book, we have sought to show some of the universal principles involved in the lucid dreaming experience that are suggestive of an objective inner psyche. We have suggested practices by which you can investigate them yourself. Moreover, we have opened up the idea of using limited and unlimited intent in lucid dreams to gain access to a second psychic system, which Jung considered of revolutionary significance in that it could radically alter our view of the world. On a practical level, we have provided examples of how experienced lucid dreamers have used their skills to promote emotional and physical healing, to gain access to creativity for the arts and science, to explore the limits of inner awareness, and to encourage transcendent experiences.

Much like electricity 200-plus years ago, lucid dreaming carries extraordinary possibilities for advancing science, the culture, and individual lucid dreamers. When it is better understood and accepted, its practical uses seem likely to flourish due to its adaptability to almost any interest or endeavor. On a theoretical level, lucid dreaming may prove to be the revolutionary tool that finally allows for a conscious exploration of what we currently call the unconscious (although it seems utterly conscious and aware). Thus, it may offer mankind an acceptable path to a more creative, integrated awareness.

You may not realize it as you inwardly explore in lucid dreams, but you may naturally integrate your conscious and unconscious mind as you personally experience the hybrid state of consciousness that neurophysiologists noted in their EEG research on lucid dreaming. Like other pioneers before you, this integration and exploration can lead you to a newfound respect for both lucid dreaming and for the creativity of the unconscious. Furthermore, it may liberate you from errant viewpoints and cultural beliefs to show you the true beauty, wonder, and depth of the psyche and your self.

Realization as Liberation

In workshops on mindfulness, you sometimes hear the saying "Realization is liberation" or "Self-realization is liberation."

A sudden remarkable realization also occurs at the moment of lucid dreaming: *I know I dream this*. In that instance, you see your experience from an expanded perspective and, in some sense, a more liberated perspective. But in what ways does that new perspective liberate you?

During lucid realization, you often feel liberation from fear. If you see a nightmarish figure like Frankenstein, you know you have nothing external to fear from him. In other cases, lucidly facing a feared object may reveal to you for the first time that you have never actually seen the feared object itself; instead, you have ignored, denied, or run from it. Seeing it lucidly may liberate you from superstitious fears and keep you from devoting your energy to your defense mechanisms—energy that you can now reclaim for more constructive pursuits.

During the lucid realization, you may feel liberation from restraints or limits, because you know you can fly and move through barriers with relative ease. Lucidity often makes apparent the possibilities for creatively influencing that which surrounds you. Although an object may appear as a barrier or a limitation, it likely exists essentially as mental energy that you can engage, manipulate and use.

Moreover, during lucid realization, you may feel the liberation of a larger knowing, because you can easily access more than your waking self and you may actively experience the vastness of your larger awareness. Using unlimited intent, you can request to understand the symbol before you, or you can request an experience beyond your waking self's knowing. You begin to understand your whole self more directly and see its connection to the ego and waking self.

As you can see, the liberating realizations characteristic of lucid dreaming have layers. One realization may seem shallow or deep, specific or general; but it often points the way to even greater depth and transformative insights. As you notice how one realization connects to or reflects on other issues, you move deeper into this liberating potential of lucidity. How far you take it depends on you and your intent, your clarity, and your powers of insight.

Realizations can definitely lead to an acceptance of a larger wholeness in which your conscious and unconscious minds begin to integrate more completely, especially when you let go of fears and limiting beliefs. Ideally, the practice of lucid dreaming should ultimately lead you to insights that illuminate how your conscious and unconscious minds work together to construct experience. Taking such insights from the lucid dreaming state to your waking life results in a new type of awareness. Lucid dreamers call this living lucidly.

Personal Integration

The concept of living lucidly expresses the idea of integrating the larger awareness and realizations experienced in lucid dreams into your waking physical reality. Because lucid dreaming shows the triumph of critical awareness over a primary assumption[126]—that your experienced reality actually exists as a dream—and reveals how the largely invisible projected mental overlay of thoughts, feelings, beliefs, expectations, and intent radiates onto your perceived experience, it encourages you to examine your assumptions and projections more clearly while awake, allowing you to live lucidly.

Remember how the woman with cheap rented wings flew around her dreamscape until she realized that only her belief in the power of the wings led to successful dream flying? In waking, she recalled this lucid dream principle when unsettled by her job interview and decided to assume a stronger belief in herself when questioned. Her new confidence and positive belief in herself allowed her to stop projecting self-defeating thoughts and obtain her goal of a job. In that moment, she experienced living lucidly.

Remember PasQuale, who ran from the Nazi soldier until she became lucid and then called out to see who was really chasing her? She learned that she was actually running from her fear of the unknown and immediately understood how this affected her waking life. She learned that running from fears will not resolve them, but only postpone another encounter. Through lucid dreaming, she learned that facing fears often leads to their immediate resolution. After she saw how her fear was limiting her and had no real basis, she resolved to change her waking-life response. In those moments of awareness, she experienced living lucidly.

Remember when I felt someone behind me in the lucid dream, picked her up, and then asked: "Who are you?" She responded: "A discarded aspect of yourself." When I decided to accept her as such with complete sincerity, she shrank down into wisps of colored light that entered my torso and gave me a jolt of energy. A week later in waking life, I suddenly realized that I did have new energy and the intent to finish my first book, a project I had discarded a few years earlier as impossible. In that moment, the energy released from that earlier blockage powered a new level of creativity, and I experienced living lucidly.

Living lucidly can help liberate you from unexamined assumptions and unnoticed projections—the constraining effects of your waking fears, limiting beliefs, unproductive expectations, and habitual intents. It can show you that these same liberating principles (which seem so obvious in lucid dreaming) often apply to your waking life as well. Living lucidly can offer you openings that allow new creativity, fulfillment, and growth by truly examining your thoughts, feelings, beliefs, expectations, and intent in the moment and seeing how these are reflected in your experience.

When you approach living lucidly, you see that much of the real work seems to be inner work; the outer situation serves as an important reminder or reflective feedback on and guide to inner issues.

Encountering an aggressive figure in the waking state, you wonder (as in a lucid dream) whether it exists as a possible reflection of some issue, conflict, or belief inside of you. Considering that, you search inwardly for how and where it may connect and what kind of response (hopefully one filled with compassion and understanding) can satisfactorily resolve it. As you look inward, these two perspectives often come together, and you suddenly know what inner change or response needs expression to resolve and integrate these energies. Your expression of these changes frequently results in reflective feedback, which shows you how the inner system responds to your actions.

Many lucid dreamers discover that these lessons in lucidity apply or generalize to both the dream and waking states. They notice that the projected power of expectation and belief in lucid dreaming shares a correspondence with their unnoticed projected expectations, assumptions, and beliefs about events or people in their waking lives. Like the teachers whose expectations were elevated when they were told that their students seemed poised for incredible growth, you consciously see how you can either live up to new and higher expectations that you truly believe in or, conversely, live down to new and lower expectations that you truly believe in. You begin to see how your beliefs and expectations guide your actions.

Throughout this book, we have included many practices to encourage lucid dreaming. Now we share one for living lucidly. Done properly, it can powerfully demonstrate the connection between your inner life, your projected mental overlay, and your reflective waking reality. You do not need to dream or lucid dream to perform this practice. If you begin to play with these neutral personality characteristics and mentally empower them, you will shortly see how all of us act as projectors, unconsciously and consciously. Through various subtle actions, we all project our focused, energized mental overlay outward onto our experience. Incredibly, the outer world responds and confirms this process.

How to Energize a Waking Belief

- Pick some personal aspect or characteristic about which you feel basically neutral. In fact, it may seem so neutral that you rarely even think about it in relation to yourself. For example, you may think you are not very funny or comedic, although you do have moments when you seem a little bit funny. Or you may feel neutral about how physically attractive you are. Whatever characteristic you select, be sure you feel truly neutral and indifferent about it.

- See that neutral characteristic as a neutral belief that you will now begin to project mental energy onto in order to help it grow and evolve. Agree to tell yourself about ten times a day how you now have that characteristic in abundance. You may say:, "I am the funniest man in this town. People find me utterly hilarious and laugh hysterically when they hear me say something." You may say to yourself ten times a day,: "I am now vivacious and attractive to the opposite sex. They find me incredibly good looking and alluring."

- Take a minute to imagine others responding to your new energized belief. See or hear them laughing at your funny statement or commenting on your radiant appearance. Do not tell anyone what you are doing.

- Tell yourself about your newly empowered characteristic about ten times a day for a minute or so. Dramatize it in your mind. Have fun with it. Allow yourself to accept the feeling of this characteristic.

- After a few days, notice how the waking world responds. Do you hear people laughing uproariously when you say something that doesn't strike you as very funny at all? Do not try to figure it out. Just begin to notice how often the world responds to you by commenting on or approving of this newly energized characteristic.

- Affirm the characteristic in your mind on a regular basis. See how the process of changing a lucid dream by changing your belief and expectations can also show you one method to change your waking experience.

By using a neutral characteristic in this practice, you can project energy onto it much more easily, because you really do not have any conflicting issues about it. (Is it moral? Will this hurt my relationships?) A neutral issue accepts mental energy easily and thus allows the change more quickly. Then, much like a lucid dream environment responding to a lucid dreamer's new expectations and beliefs, your waking world will begin to respond to your newly projected expectation and belief about the neutral issue you have begun to energize.

By contrast, a difficult emotional issue or relationship that you think about all the time and feel very upset about has a lot of mental energy already connected to it. When you decide to project a completely new type of expectation or mental energy onto this difficult issue, it often results in little immediate change due to the energetic resistance. By understanding this point, you can begin to work first on neutral personal characteristics, neutral issues at home or the office, and neutral interpersonal relationships. Empower them privately in your mind; then see the results. After you realize that this works for neutral issues, you can move forward by degree into more challenging issues or relationships.

Know Thyself

Living lucidly shows that you cannot understand your waking (or dreaming) experience without examining your assumptions and projections, and the contents of your conscious mind. As modern physics suggests, you, the observer, matter. As an observer, you can hardly remove yourself from the equation of your experience, any more than a dreamer can remove him or herself from the events of a dream.

When you begin to live lucidly, you may experience interesting events like unexpected synchronicities. Jung coined the term *synchronicity* to suggest "the simultaneous occurrence of two meaningfully but not causally connected events."[127] As a personal example, Jung pointed to a therapy session when a difficult client talked about a dream in which someone offered her a golden scarab. Suddenly, Jung heard a tapping at the window, opened it, and allowed a gold-green scarab-like beetle in. He caught the beetle and handed it to her, saying: "Here is your scarab."

Jung—who interacted with Wolfgang Pauli, one of the founders of quantum theory—felt that synchronicities suggest some underlying framework to reality or hint at the possibility of some type of interconnected collective unconscious. In *The Interpretation of Nature and the Psyche*, co-edited with Pauli, Jung writes that synchronicity "means the simultaneous occurrence of a certain [mental] state with one or more external events which appear as meaningful parallels to the momentary subjective state."[128] If you actively use the practice given above, you may see that energizing a neutral belief state can often prompt synchronistic external events suggestive of an underlying interconnected framework or hidden order.

Although this book shows beginners how to achieve lucidity, comprehend the nature of the lucid dream state, and maneuver within it, it also builds an introductory foundation for a much deeper and more thoughtful investigation into the nature of self and experienced reality. To that end, we have reframed much of the lucid dream experience into an investigation of mental energy, radiating outward from sources like the dreamer and the dreamer's larger awareness, reflecting within the dream, and leading to a type of dynamic communication within the overall psyche. Reframing lucid dreaming as an investigation of mental energy may introduce and establish a new field within consciousness studies of mental physics.

However, when you reach the dream realization that you seem largely surrounded by the formed mental energy of your own projections, you may wonder what lies beyond it. Consider this excerpt from a lucid dream[129] of Caroline's in which she uses unlimited intent to ask to have an experience beyond her projections:

> For example, I was in a lucid dream scene when I shouted to the sky, "Show me the consciousness that is beyond my projections." I was instantly sucked up through the universe and all around me the planets and the stars were shown to me

as balls of pure light and consciousness. There was no matter, just light, and the light was consciousness itself. This felt so physically real that it still gives me goose bumps thinking about it. As I hurtled through space, a male voice was repeating over and over, "The micro is the same as the macro."

I went beyond the "edge" of our universe and was surrounded by orbs of pure conscious light, which were much more densely concentrated consciousness than the planets and stars. As I went higher and higher, the orbs of light became more and more prevalent until there were so many that they were starting to fuse together, emitting more and more light. It was truly beautiful. Above me, there was nothing but pure light and unified consciousness.

Dreaming and lucid dreaming allow you to explore the inner dimensions of awareness to gain new insights on waking perception and the nature of experience—even taking the first steps to go beyond your own projections. By exploring the subconscious and unconscious foundation upon which consciousness rests, you may come to a deeper understanding of the actual nature of awareness, the nature of personal reality. As Jung paradoxically put it, "Who looks outside, dreams; who looks inside wakes."

The length, depth, and luminosity of your lucid dreaming path depend on you, your practice, and your response to unfolding realizations. As travelers who continue to explore this path and learn from it, we wish you well on your journey of awareness.

ENDNOTES

Introduction

1. Robert Waggoner, *Lucid Dreaming: Gateway to the Inner Self* (Needham, MA: Moment Point Press, 2009), p. 17.

Chapter 1

2. Keith Hearne, "Lucid dreams: An electro-physiological and psychological study." Unpublished doctoral dissertation (1978). University of Liverpool, UK.

3. Quoted in "Conscious dreaming" by Chandra Shekhar, *Science News* (Santa Barbara: University of California, 2006). *http://nasw.org/users/chandra/Clips/lucid_dreaming.htm*.

4. Stephen LaBerge, "Lucid dreaming as a learnable skill: A case study," *Perceptual and Motor Skills* 51, no. 3, pt 2, (1980), pp 1039–1042.

5. Stephen LaBerge, *Lucid Dreaming* (Los Angeles: Tarcher, 1985), p. 66.

6. Ursula Voss, Romain Holzmann, Inka Tuin, and J. Allan Hobson, "Lucid dreaming: A state of consciousness with features of both waking and non-lucid dreaming sleep," *Sleep* 32, no. 9 (September 1, 2009), pp. 1191–1200.

7. Max-Planck-Gesellschaft, "Lucid dreamers help scientists locate the seat of meta-consciousness in the brain," *Science Daily* (July 27, 2012).

9. Martin Dresler, Renate Wehrle, Victor I. Spoormaker, Stefan P. Koch, Florian Holsboer, Axel Steiger, Hellmuth Obrig, Philipp G. Sämann, and Michael Czisch, "Neural correlates of dream lucidity obtained from contrasting lucid versus non-lucid REM sleep: A combined EEG/fMRI case study," *Sleep* 35, no. 7 (2012), pp. 1017–1020.

10. Daniel Erlacher, Michael Schredl, Tsuneo Watanabe, Jun Yamana, and Florian Gantzert, "The incidence of lucid dreaming within a Japanese university student sample," *International Journal of Dream Research* 1, no. 2 (October 2008).

11. Michael Schredl, Josie Henley-Einion, and Mark Blagrove, "Lucid dreaming in children: The UK Library Study," *International Journal of Dream Research* 5, no. 1 (April 2012).

12. Ursula Voss, Clemens Frenzel, Judith Koppehele-Gossel, and J. Allan Hobson, "Lucid dreaming: An age-dependent brain dissociation," *Journal of Sleep Research* 21, no. 6 (December 2012), pp. 634–642.

13. Jayne Gackenbach and Jane Bosveld, *Control Your Dreams* (New York: Harper & Row, 1989), p. 113.

14. J. Gackenbach, N. Heilman, S. Boyt, and S. LaBerge, "The relationship between field independence and lucid dreaming ability," *Journal of Mental Imagery* 9 (1985), pp. 9–20.

15. Line Salvesen, DreamSpeak interview, *The Lucid Dream Exchange*, December 2008, vol. 49.

16. Tad Messenger, DreamSpeak interview, *Lucid Dreaming Experience* (ISSN 2167-616X) 1, no. 1 (June 2012).

17. Melanie Schädlich and Daniel Erlacher, "Applications of lucid dreams: An online study," *International Journal of Dream Research* 5, no. 2 (Oct. 2012).

18. Deirdre Barrett, *The Committee of Sleep* (New York: Crown Publishers, 2001).

19. Larry Page, Transcript of 2009 Commencement Address to the University of Michigan. *http://googlepress.blogspot.com/2009/05/larry-pages-university-of-michigan.html*.

20. Dustyn Lucas, personal communication.

21. Stephen LaBerge and Howard Rheingold, *Exploring the World of Lucid Dreaming* (New York: Ballantine Books, 1990), p. 178.

22. DreamSpeak interview; originally appeared in the March 2011 issue of *The Lucid Dream Exchange*. *http://www.dreaminglucid.com/issues/LDE58.pdf.*

23. Henry Abramovitch, "The nightmare of returning home: A case of acute onset nightmare disorder treated by lucid dreaming," *Israel Journal of Psychiatry and Related Sciences*, 32, no. 2 (1995), pp. 140–145; Andrew Brylowski, "Nightmares in crisis: Clinical applications of lucid dreaming techniques," *Psychiatric Journal of the University of Ottawa* 15, no. 2 (1990), pp. 79–84; Victor I. Spoormaker, J. van den Bout, and E. J. G. Meijer, "Lucid dreaming treatment for nightmares: A series of cases," *Dreaming* 13, no. 3 (2003), pp. 181–186.

24. LaBerge, *Lucid Dreaming*, p. 90. "[O]our research indicates that dream events are closely paralleled by brain events."

25. E. W. Kellogg III, "Lucid dream healing experiences: Firsthand accounts," presented at the Association for the Study of Dreams (ASD) Conference, Santa Cruz, CA, (July 1999).

26. Kellogg, "Lucid dream healing experiences."

27. Gackenbach and Bosveld, *Control Your Dreams*, p. 113.

28. Jayne Gackenbach, "The potential of lucid dreaming for bodily healing," *Lucidity Letter* 7, no. 2 (Dec. 1988).

29. *Nightlight: The Lucidity Institute Newsletter* 1, no. 1 (Winter, 1989).

30. Paul Tholey, "Applications of lucid dreaming in sports," *Lucidity Letter* 9 (1990), pp. 6–17.

31. Daniel Erlacher and Michael Schredl, "Applied research practicing a motor task in a lucid dream enhances subsequent performance: A pilot study," *The Sports Psychologist* 24, no. 2 (June 2010), pp. 157–167.

32. Tenzin Wangyal Rinpoche, *The Tibetan Yogas of Dream and Sleep* (Ithaca, New York: Snow Lion Publications, 1998), p. 82.

Chapter 2

33. Michael Schredl and Daniel Erlacher, "Self-reported effects of dreams on waking-life creativity: An empirical study." *Journal of Psychology* 141 (2007), pp. 35–46.

34. Matthew Ebben, Anthony Lequerica, and Arthur Spielman, "Effects of pyridoxine on dreaming: A preliminary study," *Perceptual and Motor Skills* 94, no. 1 (Feb. 2002), pp.135–40.

36. "Reviewing alcohol's effects on normal sleep," *Science Daily* (January 22, 2013).

37. E. W. Kellogg III, "The lucidity continuum," *Electric Dreams* 11, no. 10 (October 2004). *http://www.improverse.com/ed-articles/kellogg/.*

38. Robert Waggoner, *Lucid Dreaming: Gateway to the Inner Self* (Needham, MA: Moment Point Press, 2009), p. 17.

Chapter 3

39. Carlos Castaneda, *Journey to Ixtlan: The Lessons of Don Juan* (New York: Pocket Books, 1974), pp. 98–100.

40. Joseph Dane and Robert Van De Castle, "A comparison of waking instruction and posthypnotic suggestion for lucid dream induction," *Lucidity Letter* 3, no. 4 (1984).

41. Jayne Gackenbach and Jane Bosveld, *Control Your Dreams* (New York: Harper & Row, 1989), p. 34.

42. Stephen LaBerge and Howard Rheingold, *Exploring the world of lucid dreaming* (New York: Ballantine Books, 1990), p. 34.

43. Tenzin Wangyal Rinpoche, *The Tibetan Yogas of Dream and Sleep* (Ithaca, New York: Snow Lion Publications, 1998), pp. 104–105.

44. Ursula Voss, Romain Holzman, Allan Hobson, Walter Paulus, Judith Koppehele-Gossel, Ansgar Klimke, and Michael A Nitsche, "Induction of self awareness in dreams through frontal low current stimulation of gamma activity," *Nature Neuroscience* 17 (May 11, 2014), pp. 810–812.

45. Stephen LaBerge, *Lucid dreaming* (Los Angeles: Tarcher, 1985), p. 140.

46. Paul Tholey, "Overview of the development of lucid dream research in West Germany," *Lucidity Letter* 8, no. 2 (Dec. 1989).

47. Beverly D'Urso, personal communication.

48. Lynne Levitan, "Get up early, take a nap, be lucid," *Nightlight* 3, no. 1 (1993).

49. Daniel Love, *Are You Dreaming?* (Exeter, UK: Enchanted Loom Publishing, 2013).

Chapter 4
50. E. W. Kellogg III, "Lucid dream healing experiences: Firsthand accounts," presented at the ASD Conference, Santa Cruz, CA, (July 1999).

51. Carlos Castaneda, *Journey to Ixtlan: The Lessons of Don Juan* (New York: Pocket Books, 1974), p. 112.

52. Stephen LaBerge, *Lucid Dreaming* (Los Angeles: Tarcher, 1985), pp. 120–121.

53. LaBerge, *Lucid Dreaming*, p. 117.

Chapter 5
54. Mirjam Moll, "Über den Wolken Schweben," *Mannheimer Morgen* (November 9, 2013). *http://www.morgenweb.de/nachrichten/wissenschaft/uber-den-wolken-schweben-1.1275068.*

55. Melanie Schädlich, personal communication.

56. Robert Rosenthal and Lenore Jacobsen, *Pygmalion in the Classroom: Teacher Expectation and Pupils' Intellectual Development* (New York: Holt, Rinehart and Winston, 1968).

57. Beverly D'Urso, DreamSpeak interview, *The Lucid Dream Exchange* 29, no. 30, p. 31; *http://www.durso.org/beverly/My_Lucid_Life.html.*

58. Alan Worsley, "Personal experiences in lucid dreaming," *Conscious Mind, Sleeping Brain,* eds. S. LaBerge and J. Gackenbach (New York: Springer, 1988), p. 322.

59. *Lucid Dreaming Experience* (ISSN 2167-616X) 2, no. 2 (September 2013).

60. Linda Mastrangelo, "Alice's looking glass: Exploring portals in other dimensions in lucid dreams." Presented at the International Association for the Study of Dreams (IASD) PsiBer Online Conference, (2013).

61. Richard Nesbitt, *The Geography of Thought: How Asians and Westerners Think Differently . . . and Why* (New York: Free Press, 2003).

Chapter 6

62. Paul Tholey, "Applications of lucid dreaming in sports," *Lucidity Letter* 9 (1990), pp. 6–17.

63. Tenzin Wangyal Rinpoche, *The Tibetan Yogas of Dream and Sleep* (Ithaca, New York: Snow Lion Publications, 1998), p. 123.

64. Joy Fatooh, DreamSpeak interview, *The Lucid Dream Exchange*, March 2008.

65. Ursula Voss, Clemens Frenzel, Judith Koppehele-Gossel, and J. Allan Hobson, "Lucid dreaming: An age-dependent brain dissociation," *Journal of Sleep Research*, 21, no. 6 (December 2012), pp. 634–642.

66. Nigel Hamilton, *Awakening through Dreams: The Journey through the Inner Landscape* (London: Karnac Publishing, 2014).

67. Oleksandr Savsunenko, "Findings of lucid dreamers in the Ukraine." Presented at the International Association for the Study of Dreams Conference, Chicago, IL, June 2009.

68. Justina Lasley, *Honoring the Dream: A Handbook for Dream Group Leaders* (DreamsWork, 2004).

Chapter 7

69. Robert Waggoner, *Lucid Dreaming: Gateway to the Inner Self,* (Needham, MA: Moment Point Press, 2009), pp. 17–18.

70. Paul Tholey, "Consciousness and abilities of dream characters observed during lucid dreaming," *Perceptual and Motor Skills* 68, no. 2 (1989), pp. 567–578.

71. Tadas Stumbrys, Daniel Erlacher, and Steffen Schmidt, "Lucid dream mathematics: An explorative online study of arithmetic abilities of dream characters," *International Journal of Dream Research* 4, no. 1 (2011), 35–40.

72. Tadas Stumbrys and Michael Daniels. "An exploratory study of creative problem solving in lucid dreams: Preliminary findings and methodological considerations," *International Journal of Dream Research* 3, no. 2 (2010).

73. Paul Tholey, "Overview of the development of lucid dream research in West Germany," *Lucidity Letter* 8, no. 2 (Dec. 1989).

74. Tholey, "Overview of the development of lucid dream research."

75. Tholey, "Consciousness and abilities of dream characters," pp. 567–578.

76. Tholey, "Overview of the development of lucid dream research."

77. Tholey, "Overview of the development of lucid dream research."

78. Frederik van Eeden, "A study of dreams," proceedings of the Society for Psychical Research, 26 (1913).

Chapter 8

79. Denise J. Cai, Sarnoff Mednick, Elizabeth M. Harrison, Jennifer Kanady, and Sara Mednick, "Proceedings of the National Academy of Sciences," (June 23, 2009), pp. 10130–10134.

80. Ullrich Wagner, Steffen Gais, Hilde Haider, Rolf Verleger, and Jan Born, "Sleep inspires insight," *Nature* 427 (January 22, 2004), pp. 352–355.

81. Stephen LaBerge, *Lucid Dreaming* (Los Angeles: Tarcher, 1985), p. 239.

82. LaBerge, *Lucid Dreaming*, p. 244.

83. LaBerge, *Lucid Dreaming*, p. 245.

84. Mary Ziemer, DreamSpeak interview, *Lucid Dreaming Experience* (ISSN 2167-616X) 1, no. 4 (March 2013).

85. Stephen LaBerge, *Lucid Dreaming: A Concise Guide to Awakening in Your Dreams and in Your Life* (Louisville, CO: Sounds True, 2009), p. 65.

86. Carl G. Jung, "The relations between the ego and the unconscious," in *The Basic Writings of C. G. Jung*, ed. Violet Staub de Laszlo (New York: Random House, 1993), p. 196.

87. Jung, *Basic Writings*, pp. 196–197.

88. Robert Waggoner, *Lucid Dreaming: Gateway to the Inner Self* (Needham, MA: Moment Point Press, 2009), p. 146.

Chapter 9

89. PasQuale Ourtane, DreamSpeak interview, *The Lucid Dream Exchange* 42 (March 2007).

90. Paul Tholey, "A model of lucidity training as a means of self-healing and psychological growth," in *Conscious Mind, Sleeping Brain*, eds. J. Gackenbach and S. LaBerge (New York: Plenum, 1988), pp. 263–287.

91. David L. Kahn, *A Dream Come True: Simple Techniques for Dream Interpretation and Precognitive Dream Recognition* (New York: Cosimo Books, 2007).

92. Anonymous lucid dream that originally appeared in the September 2011 issue of *The Lucid Dream Exchange* 60, pp. 20–21.

93. G. Scott Sparrow, "Lucid dreaming: A path of transcendence or transformation, or both?" Presented at the annual conference of the International Association for the Study of Dreams, Asheville, North Carolina, July 1, 2010.

94. Eckhart Tolle, *A New Earth: Awakening to Your Life's Purpose* (New York: Dutton, 2005), p. 275.

95. Kelly Frappier, "Funny faces (lucid dream)," *Lucid Dreaming Experience* (ISSN 2167-616X) 1, no. 4 (March 2013), p. 36.

Chapter 10

96. Reference for this story is at *www.pbs.org/wgbh/amex/telephone/peopleevents/mabell.html.*

97. Stephen LaBerge, *Lucid Dreaming* (Los Angeles: Tarcher, 1985), pp. 66–67.

98. E. W. Kellogg III, "A lucid dream incubation technique," *Dream Network Bulletin* 5, no. 4 (1986), p. 16.

99. E. W. Kellogg III, "The lucid dream information technique," *The Lucid Dream Exchange* (December 2004).

100. Jeffrey A. Peck, Jr., personal communication.

101. D. Barrett, "Just how lucid are lucid dreams?" *Dreaming* 2, no. 4 (December 1992), pp. 221–228.

Chapter 11

102. Line Salvesen, DreamSpeak interview, *The Lucid Dream Exchange* 49 (December 2008).

103. Line Salvesen, personal communication.

104. M. Desseilles and C. Duclos, "Dream and emotion regulation: Insight from the ancient art of memory." *Behavioral and Brain Sciences* 36, no. 6 (December 2013), p. 614.

105. S. Westermann, F. M. Paulus, L. Müller-Pinzler, and S. Krach, "Elaborative encoding during REM dreaming as prospective emotion regulation," *Behavioral and Brain Sciences* 36, no. 6 (December 2013), pp. 631–633.

106. Andrew Weil, *Spontaneous Healing* (New York: Knopf, 1995), p. 4.

107. Edward Tick, *The Practice of Dream Healing* (Wheaton, IL: Quest Books, 2001), p. 156.

108. Caz Coronel, "Healing tinnitus in a lucid dream," *Lucid Dreaming Experience* (ISSN 2167-616X) 2, no. 2 (September 2013), pp. 40–41.

109. Coronel, "Healing tinnitus in a lucid dream."

Chapter 12

110. Maria Isabel Pita, "Lucid therapy: Healing my tendonitis," *Lucid Dreaming Experience* (ISSN 2167-616X) 1, no. 1 (June 2012), pp. 17–21. Visit Maria's blog at *www.lucidlivingluciddreaming.org.*

111. Robert Haskell, "Dreaming, cognition, and physical illness: Part I," *The Journal of Medical Humanities and Bioethics* 6, no. 1, pp. 46–56.

112. M. Dresler, S. P. Koch, R. Wehrle, V. I. Spoormaker, F. Holsboer, A. Steiger, P. G. Sämann, H. Obrig, and M. Czisch, "Dreamed movement elicits activation in the sensorimotor cortex," *Current Biology* 21, no. 21 (November 8, 2011), pp. 1833–1837.

113. Stephen LaBerge, *Lucid Dreaming* (Los Angeles: Tarcher, 1985), p. 86.

114. *Lucid Dreaming Experience* (ISSN 2167-616X) 2, no. 3 (December 2013), pp. 29–33.

115. Mauro Zappaterra, Lysander Jim, Sanjog Pangarkar, "Chronic pain resolution after a lucid dream: A case for neural plasticity?" *Medical Hypotheses* 82, no. 3 (March 2014), pp. 286–290.

116. M. K. Bhasin, J. A. Dusek, B-H Chang, M. G. Joseph, J. W. Denninger, et al., "Relaxation response induces temporal transcriptome changes in energy metabolism, insulin secretion and inflammatory pathways," *PLoS ONE* 8, no. 5 (2013): e62817. doi:10.1371/journal.pone.0062817.

117. B. Klopfer, "Psychological variables in human cancer," *Journal of Projective Techniques*, 21, no. 4 (December 1957), pp. 331–340.

118. Klopfer, "Psychological variables." This is one of more than 3,500 case studies that can be found in the Spontaneous Remission Project, a database compiled from medical literature by the Institute of Noetic

Sciences of cases of patients who have recovered from supposedly incurable illnesses.)

119. *The Nature of Hypnosis*, The British Psychological Society, March 2001.

120. Robert Waggoner, *Lucid Dreaming: Gateway to the Inner Self*, (Needham, MA: Moment Point Press, 2009), p. 168.

Chapter 13

121. Kristen E. LaMarca, "Lucid dream meditation," *Lucid Dreaming Experience* 48 (September 2008), p. 15.

122. LaMarca, "Lucid dream meditation."

123. Britta K. Hölzel, James Carmody, Karleyton C. Evans, Elizabeth A. Hoge, Jeffery A. Dusek, Lucas Morgan, Roger K. Pitman, and Sara W. Lazar, "Stress reduction correlates with structural changes in the amygdala," *Social Cognitive and Affective Neuroscience*, 2009.

124. S. W. Lazar, G. Bush, R. L. Gollub, G. L. Fricchione, G. Khalsa, and H. Benson, "Functional brain mapping of the relaxation response and meditation," *NeuroReport* 11 (2000), pp. 1581–1585; 16 (2000), pp. 1893–1897.

125. Britta K. Hölzel, James Carmody, Mark Vangela, Christina Congletona, Sita M. Yerramsettia, Tim Gard, and Sara W. Lazar, "Mindfulness practice leads to increases in regional brain gray matter density," *Psychiatry Res* (2010).

126. "Regulation of gene expression by yoga, meditation and related practices: A review of recent studies," *Asian Journal of Psychiatry* 6, no. 1 (February 2013), pp. 74–77.

127. Bethany E. Kok and Barbara L. Fredrickson, "Upward spirals of the heart: Autonomic flexibility as indexed by vagal tone, reciprocally and prospectively predicts positive emotions and social connectedness," *Biological Psychology* 85, no. 3, p. 432.

Chapter 14

128. E. W. Kellogg III, "Lucid dreaming and the phenomenological epoché," oral paper presentation at the Society for Phenomenology and the Human Sciences Conference in Eugene, OR, in October, 1999.

129. C. G. Jung, "Synchronicity: An acausal connecting principle," in *The Interpretation of Nature and the Psyche*, eds. Wolfgang Pauli and C. G. Jung (New York: Pantheon Books, 1955).

130. Jung and Pauli, "Synchronicity."

131. Caroline McCready, DreamSpeak interview, *Lucid Dreaming Experience* (ISSN 2167-616X) 2, no. 1 (June 2013).

ABOUT THE AUTHORS

ROBERT WAGGONER is a past president of the International Association for the Study of Dreams (IASD) and a graduate of Drake University with a degree in psychology. He is the co-editor of the online journal *Lucid Dreaming Experience* and is a frequent speaker at national and international dream conferences. He is the author of *Lucid Dreaming: Gateway to the Inner Self.* Visit Robert online at *www.lucidadvice.com.*

CAROLINE MCCREADY teaches art, meditation, lucid dreaming, and creativity workshops in London. She has a BA honors degree from the University of Warwick, studied sculpture in London and has an SQC in Psychology from Oxford Brookes University. For more information visit *www.carolinemccready.com.*

To Our Readers

Conari Press, an imprint of Red Wheel/Weiser, publishes books on

al growth, and relationships to
ues. Our mission is to publish
in people's lives—how we feel
another. We value integrity,
ooks we publish and in the

esource, and we appreciate
what you would like to see

iser.com to learn about our
d be sure to go to www.
r newsletters and exclusive

oks.com.